The People's College, Its Contributions and Its Application to American Education and Conditions

Paul Henry Holm-Jensen, Ph. D.
Luverne, North Dakota

Blair, Nebraska
1939

Copyright 1939

Danish Lutheran Publishing House
Blair, Nebraska

Dedication

TO KING CHRISTIAN X AND THE PEOPLE
OF DENMARK, BY WHOSE EXAMPLE IN
DEMOCRATIC IDEALS, GOOD WILL, AND
UNDERSTANDING, GREAT ACHIEVEMENTS
HAVE BEEN MADE WITH FEW MEANS,
THIS VOLUME IS HUMBLY DEDICATED.

Poet is every man, who in
Classroom, courtroom or church,
In wealth or lowliness,
Can see the ideal behind his task.

—Ludvig Schrøder.

Table of Contents

Page

Introduction 9

Two Problems in American Education.................. 13

The Founders of the People's College.................. 30

The People's College 57

Contribution of the People's College
1. Community Education 72
2. Scientific Farming............................. 83
3. Cooperatives.................................. 90

History of Danish Folk High Schools in America.......108

American Folk Schools................................132

Folk Schools in European Countries..................156

The Application 165

Diagram—The School System of Denmark.............186

Appendix 187

Bibliography 191

Introduction

In recent years some educators, John Dewey, Willard N. Givens, Robert Maynard Hutchins, Fred J. Kelly, John E. Stout, and others, have voiced their dissatisfaction with secondary education and higher learning in America. Some have maintained, and with good reasons, that higher education (education above the sixth grade) has failed to give what the masses really needed. Others have held that education has failed by trying to follow the rapid strides of mechanical progress.

Many sincere educators, alarmed by the great number of unemployed and the enormous amount of released human energy being wasted, have looked for **something** that would overcome the deficiencies in our mass education. It is generally conceded that higher education has been too professional in character and that a more liberal and cultural type of education should be made available.

Apparently there is a need of reconstruction in the educational organizations. This concerns especially the junior high school and the junior college. The curriculum needs also a reconstruction which would provide non-technical, integrated, survey and orientation courses that would have one main aim—the cultural development of the individual rather than the professional.

In this volume the attempts at solution of some of the problems in American education will be based upon the People's College, which originated in Denmark in 1844.

The place of origin might be a hindrance to some, since this system of cultural education did not originate in America. Mr. Hart seems to be conscious of this when he writes in his book, "Light from the North":

There is a certain type of provincial American who spends much energy in decrying "foreign" ideas and movements and in insisting that "American ideas" are good enough for America. But the fact is that it is often difficult to trace the origins of an idea. For instance, were Booker T. Washington's ideas, as developed at Tuskegee Institute, American? Was the "Literary Society" of the country school districts of Indiana a half century ago an American idea? Is the Chautauqua Movement of today an American idea? Are "finishing schools" for young ladies American? Is the Y. M. C. A. summer school an American idea? Are Harvard and Yale American products?"[1]

The Great Teacher of old said: "No man liveth unto himself." This truth applies well to education. Nations have much to learn from each other. Joseph K. Hart, Paul Monroe, and others believe that we in America have much to learn in adult education from the Danish Folk Schools and that we should not hesitate to apply the Folk School principles of democratic Denmark to the problems in America.

Rural America is in need of educational opportunities. In the agricultural state of North Dakota there are nine professional institutions of higher learning as compared with three agricultural schools preparing country youth for their tasks. It is the author's contention that secondary schools should be provided for the youth of the farm communities. Some successful attempts have been made in America, as for example at the College of Agriculture, University of Wisconsin, Park River and Maddock Agricultural Schools, North Dakota; John C. Campbell Folk School, Brasstown, North Carolina; and Danebod Folk High School, Tyler, Minnesota.

[1] Joseph K. Hart, "Light from the North," pp. IX, X.

Much difficulty was encountered in collecting historical material for the Danish Folk Schools in America and other countries as some of the schools for various reasons no longer exist. The writer is grateful to the many who answered questionnaires and personal letters and who freely gave of their time for interviews. The writer is indebted to Dr. Martin Hegland, Mrs. Olive D. Campbell, Miss Myrtle E. Pedersen, Miss Josephine Sandvig, the Rev. P. C. Jensen, editor of Luthersk Ugeblad, my two brothers, Oscar and Valdemar, and to my beloved wife, Dorthea, for their encouragement to collect the information for this thesis.

The writer expresses his appreciation to educators in many countries for their hospitality and assistance, and to the many friends for their help and encouragement. Above all, the writer is indebted to the Committee of the Graduate Division of the University of North Dakota, whose suggestions and comments were so valuable. The writer is particularly indebted to Dean J. V. Breitwieser, Director of the Graduate Division; Dr. Erich Selke, Chairman of the Committee; Dr. Richard Beck, Dr. C. L. Kjerstad, Dr. A. V. Overn, and Dr. Clarence Perkins.

Since this manuscript was first prepared for and approved by the Committee of the Graduate Division of the University of North Dakota, many changes have been made. The writer assumes full responsibility for the entire manuscript.

CHAPTER I

TWO PROBLEMS IN AMERICAN EDUCATION

I. Introduction to the Problems.—Since the writer more than a decade ago first came in personal contact with education in America, he has observed that educational institutions, teachers, and students in America have to face many serious problems. That America has problems in education, a glance at the headlines of the Sunday edition of a metropolitan newspaper will soon verify. The headlines read: "Educators Debate Propaganda Peril"; "Dewey States Aim of 'Progressives'"; "College Seniors 'Forgotten Men'"; "Johns Hopkins Puts Limit on Students"; "Conference to Study Amusement Trend."[1]

Social and other conditions in America have changed during the last decade. The abundance of technically trained men and women has created a serious problem. The demand for professional service has not increased proportionally with the number of graduates. Hence, an acute situation has arisen.

Attendance at higher institutions of learning has increased enormously, as the following quotation shows:

> Japan heads the list with an increase of 636 per cent between 1913 and 1934, closely followed by Roumania with an increase of 570 per cent. The increase in British India has been 290 per cent. Similar though less substantial gains have been made in France (112 per cent), Holland (145 per cent), Great Britain (82 per cent), and in the United States (200 per cent). Student enrollments in German institutions of higher learning increased from 76,800 in 1913 to 132,000 in 1930. Since that year they have fallen again to 77,000, largely owing to National-Socialist propaganda and the drastic measures taken **by the Hitler government** to block the access to colleges and universities.[2]

---

[1] "New York Times," March 6, 1938.
[2] W. M. Kotschnig, "The Educational Record," July, 1937, p. 354.

American life is in a changing process and every social institution attempts to meet the demands of the time. While secondary education and higher learning have tried to meet the demands, they have contributed toward the creation of new problems. The result has been a loss in the high standard and respect formerly enjoyed by American institutions of learning. From the time of Washington to the last decade our institutions of learning have grown in an environment which demanded more and more graduates. The task was to supply teachers for new schools, engineers for railroads and bridges, architects for new constructions, and trained men and women for every type of occupation. This great demand, however, has largely come to an end.

Secondary education and higher learning in America appear to be in a serious dilemma. Educators from various types of educational institutions bear witness to this situation. Educational books and magazines, lectures in the class rooms and at teachers' conventions, discussions in the halls of our colleges and universities, parents' and teachers' meetings—all seem to indicate a restless spirit. The universities are accused of being radical, teaching foreign doctrines and isms contrary to our democratic ideals of liberty and equality. Moral standards and moral ideals seem to be a matter of individual responsibility instead of institutional. The unique and lofty ideals of our forefathers have partly been lost in our present day mass education. This, in short, appears to be the prevailing situation in America today.

That America has very serious educational problems is expressed in a survey made in 1933 by a certain high school which discussed plans for the celebration of the Tercentenary of Secondary Education. During the discussion a member of the school suggested that rather than have a program, they deal with problems which the high school system has failed to solve during its 300 years of existence. Two problems were chosen for study:

First, the problem of the young people of high school age who are not enrolled in high school. Arising under this heading were such questions as the following:

1. What proportion of young people of high school age are not enrolled in Central high school?

2. How many of the young people not enrolled are unemployed?

3. How many of the young people not enrolled are following no systematic plan for study and self-improvement?

4. What could the school do to extend its services to these young people?

Second, the problem of the graduates of the high school who have not found employment. Under this we might ask:

1. How many of the graduates of the last five years are not attending college and are not employed?

2. What new employment opportunities could the community provide?

3. What is Central high school doing to serve the post-graduate?[1]

The survey subsequently made by this high school showed that about half of the boys and girls eligible for high school were not enrolled. Of those graduated the last five years, only half had employment. The other half was distributed in the Citizens' Civilian Corps, listed in the column, "Work Wanted," or belonged to that mobile population called "hobos." A few were found behind prison bars. This is the lamentable situation prevailing among the youth of America today.

In January, 1935, Joy Elmer Morgan, editor of "The Journal of the National Education Association," wrote:

The Tercentenary of Secondary Education finds millions of young people out of school and out of work. Youth stands waiting at the gates ready, willing, eager! Shall it be denied its opportunity? Dare it be denied its opportunity? Just as the acorn lodged in a rock crevasse

---

[1] Craven, Eleanor, "The Journal of the National Education Association," January, 1935, p. 19.

rends the mountains in twain with the force of its growth, so the "growth" power of oncoming millions of young men and women cannot well be resisted. Youth will have its day. From millions of young people a bitter question rises: "No schools! No jobs! What shall we do?" America must find an answer to this challenging question. During the Tercentenary year each high school ought to embrace the opportunity to devote a major share of its attention to a study of the unemployed youth of its community and to the discovery of ways by which the high school may extend its services to them.[1]

The problem, instead of being solved, has increased to the point where a large proportion of our youth are becoming desperate for something creative to occupy their minds and bodies. A recent report published by the Welfare Council in New York City shows a most alarming situation:

Nearly half of the young men and women in this city are suffering from lack of economic opportunity, the Greater New York Fund reported yesterday on the basis of a study just completed by the Welfare Council. A sampling of one per cent of the population between the ages of sixteen and twenty-four indicated that about **400,000 young New Yorkers were unable to find jobs.**

"This situation challenges the resources of every agency in the community," said Winthrop Rockefeller, executive vice chairman of the fund, which will seek $10,-000,000 next month in behalf of private social groups.

"Experienced social workers agree that it may be only a short step from youthful discouragement to youthful delinquency. Yet many welfare and health agencies, which comprise with us the Greater New York Fund and are devoted to guiding the city's youth, find their resources badly strained."

The sampling made by the Welfare Council was believed to be "a fair cross-section of all social, economic, racial and cultural groups in the city and hence to represent conditions in **all classes** of the population." The percentage of youth unemployment for the city as a whole was put at 47.8.[2]

Youth is the period of developing character and of unfolding personality. Youth wants to give expression

---

[1] Morgan, Joy Elmer, "The Journal of the National Education Association," January, 1935, p. 19.

[2] "New York Times," April 3, 1938.

to its creative imagination and ideas in employment that is useful and wholesome. Youth must have an outlet for its abundant energy. This must be found in work that will bring the necessities of life, and in cultural entertainment that will satisfy the physical and mental life of the individual. With this problem in view, the task of the educator, and, in fact of every parent in America, becomes a serious one.

But mere negative criticism, too much of which has been given since the depression of 1929, is destructive. Some of the critics know little of the true meaning of education; others, to please the voters, care merely for the saving of a few dollars; still others have simply personal ambitions in view. Such forces have little good to contribute. What is needed is real constructive criticism, which does more than merely consider the inconsistencies and evils in the whole present educational scheme, a criticism which views these inconsistencies and evils in the light of possible positive solutions. It approaches each problem with an open mind, ready to grant the existence of all possible faults. It does so with understanding and sympathy, realizing the importance of the faults, but at the same time, desiring constructive improvement that will benefit the present and the coming generations. With this attitude firmly established, let us consider two of the problems in secondary education and higher learning in America today.

II. The Problem of Aims.

To the writer, the most serious criticism of American education—and of education anywhere at any time—is the lack of specific **aims**. In places, students and institutions appear to comprise one great heterogeneous group with almost as many aims as there are students and institutions. Now and then, however, a student does begin his high school work with a particular goal in view. This goal he retains through college and university; it continues in actual life. Some institutions give a reason for their existence, because they wish to make a definite contribution that improves the individual life and in turn improves America. Many institutions, however, seem to leave their students to make the best of life, relying on chance and good luck. This holds true especially in regard to morality and the leisure hours. Our almost sole concern has been, in one way or another, to give the majority of the students sufficient knowledge about a profession so as to enable them to make a living eight hours of the day during six days of the week. This has been accomplished at the expense of the leisure hours and character building.

It is generally conceded that if education is to succeed it must have specific aims. This is the opinion of a group of college presidents, deans, and office personnel representing the American Council on Education. Their ideas found expression in the following statement:

> One of the basic purposes of higher education is the preservation, transmission, and enrichment of the important elements of culture—the product of scholarship, research, creative imagination, and human experience. It is the task of colleges and universities so to vitalize this and other educational purposes as to assist the student in developing to the limit of his potentialities and in making his contribution to the betterment of society. This philosophy imposes upon educational institutions the obligation to consider the student as a whole—his intellectual capacity and achievement, his physical condition, his social relationships, his vocational aptitudes and skills, his moral and religious values, his economic resources, his aesthetic appreciation.[1]

The most commendable aim of American education today is that the masses are given an opportunity to share equally in higher learning. Ruskin, in speaking

---

[1] "The Educational Record," July, 1937, p. 431.

of education, feels that all men and women should have
a thorough and wholesome education. He says:

> I do not say, nor do I believe, that the lower classes
> ought not to be better educated, in millions of ways, than
> they are. **I believe every man in a Christian Kingdom
> ought to be equally well educated.** But I would have it
> education to purpose: stern, practical, **irresistible,** in mor-
> al habits, in bodily strength and beauty in all faculties
> of mind capable of being developed under the circum-
> stances of the individual, and especially in the technical
> knowledge of his own business; but yet, infinitely var-
> ious in its effort, directed to make one youth humble, and
> another confident; to tranquilize this mind, to put some
> spark of ambition into that; and in the doing of all this,
> considering knowledge as one only out of myriads of
> means in its hands, or myriads of gifts at its disposal.[1]

No other country offers such opportunities to the
young as America. America has more students in high
schools and colleges than the rest of the world together.
Each day millions of tomorrow's leaders are availing
themselves of the opportunity to get a liberal and scientific education, and the number is steadily increasing;
in fact, increasing so rapidly that many are becoming
alarmed. What will the future bring? Many fear that
an idle group of high school and university graduates,
who, due to their lack of a responsible position or lack
of the position for which they were prepared, will become restless, bitter, and radical. Such an educated
group of individuals is dangerous, morally and political-
ly. It was this sort of group that aided Hitler in getting
control of Germany.

If there is any place where guidance is needed, it is
in the education of the masses. A few educated radicals
are dangerous; but masses without sane and wholesome
objectives are a danger to the entire nation. If the individuals within the masses lack personal honor and
self-control, they are a danger to civilization, and a danger to society. The individual is often lost in the mass.

---

[1] Ruskin, "Stones of Venice," pp. 119, 120.

The single vote which is the individual's expression of power, is in many instances dictated. This is partly the result of mass education where personal educational guidance is lacking. The very factor, then, that has made America the outstanding country in the world, the very factor that was hoped would bring new and constant advances for better things, is rapidly becoming a dangerous force which threatens intellectual, moral, religious, political, and economic freedom. That such a situation should be the outcome of mass education few, if any, ever suspected. The cause, however, lies to a large extent in the lack of definite wholesome aims.

What has been the aim of mass education in our high schools up until the last decade? Has it been to prepare students for entrance into college and university? Or has it been to give them a taste of subjects they would not be expected to use? The situation today is not clear. As yet we have not made up our minds whether a high school education is a preparation for higher learning, or an end in itself. Some will admit the former and deny the latter, and vice versa. In other words, we have no specific aims. This makes the whole problem somewhat confusing. Confusion does appear to characterize many of our American high schools.

Dr. Hutchins believes the same confusion characterizes our higher learning, when he says:

> The college of liberal arts is partly high school, partly university, partly general, partly special. Frequently it looks like a teacher-training institution; frequently it looks like nothing at all. The degree it offers seems to certify that the student has passed an uneventful period without violating any local, state or federal law, and that he has a fair, if temporary recollection of what his teachers have said to him. As I shall show later, little pretense is made that many of the things said to him are of much importance.[1]

---

[1] Hutchins, "The Higher Learning in America," p. 2.

Who are at fault for this sad situation? The parents? It must be admitted that many parents will encourage their sons and daughters to attend college or university, although they realize that they are not capable of acquiring advanced education. Nevertheless, parents will make sacrifices in order to improve the social standing of their children and increase their opportunity for a larger income.

> An indirect proof of the validity of this situation can be found in the general tendency to replace the more difficult academic subjects by easier, more "useful" courses which are within the grasp of the "also-students." Thus, on the college level, enrollments in such courses as philosophy, mathematics, and ancient and even modern languages are nearly everywhere on the decline. In other words, those courses which are eminently fitted to give the students the essential elements of human knowledge and an understanding of first principles are forsaken. Their place is taken by purely utilitarian and vocational subjects, from bookkeeping to hotel management. At the university level both research and truly professional training, which can never be purely utilitarian, are hampered by the presence of multitudes whose general education is sketchy and who are unable to relate their specific fields to first principles.[1]

Or are the educational institutions to blame? Guided by the principles of equality, the doors to higher learning have been swung wide open, permitting practically every applicant to enter. Some institutions actually are seeking students without specifying any other qualification than that of a high school diploma. In order to maintain their "reputation," these institutions need the students and their fees. But this questionable procedure appears to be destroying the confidence which the people should have in institutions of higher learning. A large percentage of the people have lost confidence in politics and the state; if they also lose confidence in education, where shall they turn for anything unifying or

---

[1] Kotschnig, Walter M., Limiting Student Enrollments, "The Educational Record," July, 1937, p. 355.

fundamental in the state? This situation would mean a disintegration of fundamental American institutions. Since there is complete separation between church and state, the church could not act as a unifying agent. Furthermore, within the church there are denominations which could not unite on even the most fundamental questions in religion. Even if they could, it would not remedy the situation, since more than half the nation does not belong to any church at all. Thus, having no unifying agent, conditions in America would be favorable for a dictator of the Hitler type. Writing on this problem of higher education, Kotschnig says:

> We are obviously confronted here with only one of the causes leading to the rise of Hitler and other revolutionary leaders, yet it is significant that unemployed university graduates were, as leaders of the S.S. and S.A., in the vanguard of the Hitler revolution. Similarly the fascist Iron Guard in Roumania, which is responsible for the assassination of one Roumanian Prime Minister, draws its most ardent supporters from amongst unemployed, discontented graduates. The same is true of extremist movements in Holland, Belgium, France, Austria, Poland, and other countries. Frustrated and miserable, these young people and the social groups from which they come are abandoning all rational planning, which characterizes the educated person, and seek their salvation in an appeal to force. Not only are professional services diminishing in price, but the intellect itself, and education conceived as intellectual training are losing the popular esteem, are being devaluated. Intellect yields to emotional impulses stimulated by agitators and demagogues, the school as an educational agency yields to storm troops and all kinds of regimented organizations for political combat.

> There is but one conclusion to be drawn from all these phenomena: in so far as the planless expansion of higher education is leading to a lowering of standards in colleges and universities, to more unemployment of the highly educated, and for that reason not only to social unrest but to a surrender of intellectual values and a denial of the intellect, ways and means have to be found to save education from itself, to give purpose and direction to the evolution of higher learning.[1]

---

[1] "Ibid," pp. 358-359.

This does not mean that there should be no professional training given. As was pointed out at the beginning of the chapter, a certain percentage of professionally trained men and women are always needed. But, as Kotschnig says, an over-supply cheapens the professions and is dangerous to a nation's future. What is needed is more educational opportunity in various types of institutions, especially in agriculture. To quote Kotschnig again:

> Students with a strong intellectual bent, the hand-minded, and those who without being morons are not particularly able in any direction continue to be **put through** more or less **the same mill.** Most of them receive a diluted type of college preparatory education which retards those who are really fit for higher studies, and prompts many of those who are not to complete their education in an institution of higher learning. This situation is likely to persist as long as the American system of secondary education does not offer enough different types of schools or courses, each to be characterized by clearly defined educational objectives.[1]

The need of specialized training is not to be minimized. This is true especially in America, according to John Stuart Mill who says:

> The great desideratum in America—and though not quite in an equal degree, I may say in England too—is the improvement of the higher education. America surpasses all countries in the amount of mental cultivation which she has been able to make universal; but a high average level is not everything. There are wanted, I do not say a class, but a great number of persons of the highest degree of cultivation which the accumulated acquisitions of the human race make it possible to give them. From such persons in a community that know no distinction of ranks, civilization would rain down its influences on the remainder of society, and the higher faculties, having been highly cultivated in the more advanced part of the public, would give forth products and create an atmosphere that would produce a high average of the same faculties in a people so well prepared in point of general intelligence as the people of the United States.[2]

---

[1] "Ibid."
[2] Mill, "Letters," Vol. II, p. 227.

Everyone should be given an opportunity to work at the task for which he is fitted. This is the opinion of Dewey and others who write:

> In a democracy such as ours it is desirable to permit each individual to capitalize to the fullest extent on whatever interests, abilities, and potentialities he possesses. Guidance service will assist the individual in discovering his interests, abilities and potentialities; training service will assist him in preparing to enter advantageously or progress in that vocation in which he can utilize best those traits that he possesses.[1]

III. The Problem of Support.

Besides the problem of educational aims, there is the problem of **support** of educational institutions. Support of secondary schools and institutions of higher learning is derived from four sources: (1) the state, (2) donations, (3) student fees, and (4) the federal government. It was not until recently, however, that the federal government, under one of the New Deal enterprises, found it convenient to assist needy students. But this has made the support of educational institutions yet more complex. Each source has its own temporary, fixed idea concerning the goals of education, trying, through means that are often unworthy of the ideals of education, to control courses and their interpretation, to establish departments that would train students for work which no longer exists, to stress sports and "whims" of the times. All of this is often done to satisfy the "intellectually interested" who support the school. Many are the institutions that have suffered and are suffering under such regimentation. How can democratic ideas and ideals thrive and unfold themselves in such atmosphere?

The state is, in most instances the largest supporter. It is responsible for the maintenance of its own higher institutions, a responsibility which is primarily intrusted

---

[1] "Implications of Social-Economic Goals for Education," p. 69.

to the governor and a board of administration. Generally, the legislature has control of funds for the state as a unit. Outside of this power the legislature exercises little authority over individual institutions. The furtherance of education is then left to a few temporary politicians whose interests are often selfish and out of harmony with the ideals of education. Their interests may bring about reduction of support, unfortunate changes of administrative policies, and dismissing of conservative or progressive instructors as the case may be. Then again the interests of others may result in the erection of new buildings and schools; the buying of better equipment; the hiring of more and better instructors, and the establishing of new types of schools such as, science and vocational schools.

Whatever the interests may be, the question is: Is it truly democratic to intrust the education of our youth —which is for life—to a few temporary politicians, whose good will is essential for the future of tomorrow's citizens? Is it any wonder that there is confusion in purpose when education has to be ruled by the whims of the times, the educational "zeitgeist?" In this connection Ruthven says:

> For many years it has been the aim of those desirous of improving the educational opportunities of our citizens to protect these schools from their most imminent danger—partisan political influence. But while it has been the dream of educators to see state-supported colleges and universities safe from party and faction, and faculties and administrators of state schools continue to give lip service to this ideal, according to a recent report (Authority of State Executive Agencies Over Higher Education, U.S. Office of Education Bulletin, No. 15, p. 6) in only six of these schools do the governing boards now occupy a position of independence in regard to the powers of state executive officials and agencies.[1]

---

[1] A. E. Ruthven, Leadership or Regimentation in Higher Education, "The Educational Record," July, 1937, p. 347.

Another problem which has caused much confusion is **endowments** or **donations.** These are generally given by wealthy men who wish to leave a memorial for themselves. They have little special interest in education. Perhaps they were graduated from that particular institution and feel more or less obligated to express their appreciation by making a donation. Seldom does it pay for an institution to accept a new building for the upkeep of which no funds have been left. Yet administrators are anxious to get endowments. They know that an institution is largely valued educationally according to its wealth; thus, principles are often sacrificed for money, to the detriment of educational progress. Between 1902 and 1934 gifts to higher institutions from wealthy individuals and foundations amounted to 680 million dollars.[1]

As already intimated, the institutions of learning are not without a share in creating the problems of donations. Their love for money in many instances caused an increase in student fees to the extent of making educational opportunities available only for the youth of wealth. In an eastern university, after an investigation, it was found that about three-fourths of the students were from wealthy homes. These students were not primarily interested in education, but rather in social life and sports. So far, students who have been sent to college with primary interest in social activities have isolated themselves in small exclusive groups. Educationally, this is deplorable. Only a select few can participate in the life of these groups. This causes class distinction which is quite un-American in spirit. Many worthy students, due to high student fees, have been excluded from educational institutions. These students

---

[1] "New York Times," March 6, 1937.

would not form a society within society; scholarship and research would not be strangers.

To attract students, the college must have a fairly large enrollment, a substantial income, favorable location, well equipped buildings, a beautiful campus, well known professors, and courses in every thinkable field of thought and vocation. This has resulted in what Hutchins calls a "service-station conception of a university."[1]

In 1937 a measure, which would provide millions of dollars for distribution to the schools for educational purposes, was introduced in Congress. This bill is still with a committee. It has, however, been endorsed by many educational organizations. The provision is made that the allotted funds are to be without political authority and given directly to the states for distribution. Certain states as New York and California, due to their favorable locations, have larger incomes in proportion to population than other states. The profit of these two states comes largely from other states in the union. It is only fair, therefore, that through the federal government all the schools should share in this profit.

The following excerpt published by the Education News, Washington Bureau, shows the extent to which the federal government has already entered the field of education through the Works Progress Administration:

More than 190,000 individuals were enrolled in 17,195 literacy classes last October (the latest date for which figures are available); 159,430 were taking classes in vocational work; avocational and leisure time classes drew 138,226 enrollees; parent and homemaking courses attracted 136,379 individuals; college level and correspondent courses had 29,609 students; public affairs pupils number 27,249; workers' education classes accounted for 26,726 of the total; general adult education enrollees numbered 271,308; nursery school pupils totaled more than 40,000; the remaining 120,038 students in WPA

[1] Hutchins, "The Higher Learning in America, p. 6.

classes in various parts of the country were generally classified in "other" courses.[1]

This excerpt shows the attitude of the Federal government toward the educational requirements for citizenship. This attitude is apparent in a great variety of subjects. Students are of all ages and from all walks of life. The subjects as a whole, with few exceptions, are of a practical and cultural nature.

Such aid from the federal government might call for certain standards in buildings and instructors, for certain courses, and even for the establishment of new departments. If such provisions are to be attached to the bill now in Congress, the problem of support of education will be exceedingly complex. Only a policy which permits autonomy of control of education by the states and their divisions can rightly serve the nation.

The educational problem of this chapter might well be summed up in the following words by Ruthven:

> The adjustment to the conditions of a new struggle for existence which must now perforce be made by the schools requires of educators a decision which cannot be avoided. They may attempt to provide leadership through study of the problems of change and by the exercise of judgment, tact, and wisdom in the solution of these problems, or they may adopt an attitude of indifference, hopelessness, or selfishness and permit their institutions to fall into the hands of politicians and bureaucrats to be regimented by formulas and the demands for special interests. A survey of present trends of thought and action seems to discover teachers and administrators as academically inclined to one course while adopting in practice the other. School men still appear confident of their ability to guide the destinies of their institutions and continue to preach the virtues of institutional independence and academic freedom. At the same time, they are both wittingly and unwittingly very rapidly trading away their leadership, and by failure to deal effectively with their problems they are building up a strong case for a system of forced cooperation and remote control.[2]

---

[1] "New York Times," March 6, 1938.

[2] Ruthven, Alexander C., "Leadership or Regimentation in Higher Education, The Educational Record," July, 1937, p. 346.

Thus we see that the problem of support offers a serious challenge to American educators. Our aims in education will largely depend upon the sources of and the requirements attached to support. But America has men with vision, men who will tackle these problems for the good of youth, men who will deal wisely with future America.

In this general discussion of aims and support, the writer has thus far in the treatise intentionally omitted the specific problem—the problem of educating farm youth. The reason for this omission is that the same type of education, with few exceptions, has been offered to city and farm youth alike. But in the following chapters we shall consider a cultural school for farm youth—the Danish People's College, its contributions and application to the American farm community.

CHAPTER II

THE FOUNDERS OF THE PEOPLE'S COLLEGE

O day full of grace, which we behold,
Now gently to view ascending;
Thou over the earth thy reign unfold,
Good cheer to all mortals lending,
That children of light in every clime
May prove that the night is ending.
—Grundtvig.

I. Grundtvig—The Friend of Youth

Almost every national crisis in human history has produced a great leader whose personality towers above events as a city built on a hill overlooks the valley below. In the nineteenth century Grundtvig was the Light of the North. His name is indelibly written on the pages of Scandinavian history throughout that troublesome century. The depressed in spirit and body could with confidence look to him as their benefactor. Without an understanding of his life we shall miss the value and meaning of the Danish People's college movement.

Childhood.—Nicolai Frederik Severin Grundtvig, an imposing name worthy of ninety years, was born in Udby parsonage, September 8, 1783, on the island of Zealand, Denmark. This friend of the common people, this noble educator, bishop, historian, poet, and statesman descended from a long line of noble characters in Danish history. His forefathers had for three centuries held positions as city mayors and clergymen. The proud but thoughtful mother, of the renowned family of Bang, said of her new-born son:

"Skal hin sidste Trøje springe,
Blir han dog til Bogen holdt."

With the persistent help of his mother and a tutor, Grundtvig did become a student. At the age of eight he read such long, factual historical sources as "The Family History of the Danish Kings." The events and persons in these histories so caught his fancy that he never forgot them. Already at this early stage of life his interest in history and in all that was Danish had awakened only to become a silent force which spurred him onward to further historical investigation. With much profit he read Ludvig Holberg's "Church History" and "Comedies." In the former he saw the importance of Christianity to Western civilization. The latter gave him a keen sense of humor which he retained until his dying hour. With awe he read Suhm's book, "The North." These works, combined with visits by distinguished men who came regularly to the parsonage, greatly influenced young Grundtvig. It was in this atmosphere of scholarship and admiration for learning that the ambitious youth developed a lasting interest in reading.

Another experience destined to influence Grundtvig came when he, at the age of nine, was sent to a parsonage located in the beautiful country of Vejle to receive instruction from a clergyman. In these natural scenic surroundings he lived six years with "peasants and bees." The latter inspired him to meditate and write on the wisdom of God as manifested in creation. From the simple, hard-working peasants he learned that their strength was fundamentally grounded in the home and in the mother tongue.

The two years at the "dead Latin school" at Aarhus,

Grundtvig considered wasted. He accomplished little of lasting value, and it was during these years of adolescence that he lost the childlike and living relationship to Christianity and history. No longer did he have admiration and love for them.

An Indifferent Youth.—Thus, with a mind filled with impressions of compulsory church and school attendance, he entered the University of Copenhagen at the age of seventeen. According to the wishes of his parents he matriculated in the school of theology. Personally, he had lost the faith of his childhood, and, as he tells us, "it never even occurred to him to attend a church service." Surrounded by a group of happy Copenhagen friends, he lived a self-conceited and carefree life. The University left little impression on him except for the lectures of Henrik Steffens, his cousin, who introducd him to the German philosophy of Goethe, Schiller, Fichte, and Schelling. Steffens had just returned from Germany and showed much enthusiasm in the new spirited philosophy. This influence on Grundtvig was later shown in his poetry and in his interpretation of history. He was graduated with high honors but without spirit and without faith. His versatility in history, literature, and other fields was unquestioned, but his inspiration and enthusiasm had not been awakened.

The Awakening.—In 1803, an event, which was destined to change his view of the future, occurred in the life of Grundtvig. He was called to be a tutor at Egelykke, a manor on Langeland. This self-contained young man, so sure of himself, was greatly humbled by falling in love with the mistress of the house. Of this unfortunate attachment, he writes:

> Merely to realize that I was in love was enough to make me thoroughly unhappy. My humble circumstances presented an insurmountable barrier. How I struggled

against that growing passion! With all my might I forced my mind to the most difficult labors in order to quiet the storm which was raging within! But my efforts were in vain. It was like trying to dam a rushing mountain torrent with one's hands. For years, the struggle continued. Exhausted, I fell into the deepest melancholy.[1]

Describing his feelings further, he writes: "I saw a woman, and I, who had been the most cold and bitter scoffer at love, experienced now the deepest and most glowing love possible to a mortal; 'but' the civil law stood between us as an insurmountable wall, and nature had made a bottomless abyss between us."[2]

That he did not despair was due to the realization that what he needed was an awakened life. He loved her because she had succeeded in bringing him to the knowledge of that higher life. To him life became an arena where the contestants fight with the forces of good and evil. The outcome of the combat depended upon an intelligent choice.

This experience, instead of crushing him, served to awaken in him a new interest in poetry. He became a prolific writer of poems on the subjects of religion and old Norse mythology. In a few years he was recognized as the greatest Scandinavian hymn writer, being the author of more than five hundred hymns.

The Spirit of the Reformer.—Before leaving Langeland, Grundtvig had a religious experience which made him a student of the Bible. Anew he saw the Christian currents in world history unfold themselves before him. Realizing the meaning of Christianity in his own life, he felt inspired to be ordained to the ministry in order to serve the people of Denmark more profitably. A burning zeal for helping his depressed fellow men had awakened, and this was combined with a deep sense of responsibility. The fighting spirit of the reformer was

---

[1] Hollman, "The Folk High School, p. 5.
[2] Petersen and Andersen, "Illustrated Dansk Litteraturhistorie," p. 145.

coming to light. The keynote was given when he, in 1811, shortly before his ordination, delivered a trial sermon on the text, "Why has the Lord's Word Departed from His House?"

In the midst of protests and criticisms from the clergy, Grundtvig began his pastoral career, which was destined to change the life of Denmark. The Christian faith and confidence which he had regained became a dynamic motive-power in all his activities.

The power was shown in the reformer when, in 1825, a prominent professor in the department of theology at the University of Copenhagen published a religious treatise which was dominated by materialism. To this treatise Grundtvig answered at once with his "Kirkens Genmæle,"[1] wherein he rebukes the author for having lost the soul of the Danish people. As a result Grundtvig was forced to appear in court to be reprimanded for his answer. But the common people, seeing a friend in Grundtvig, praised the courage he had manifested.

During the years of 1813-1830 the ideas of a Folke-højskole (People's College) had gradually formulated into specific conceptions. After 1830 he began to give definite expression regarding the establishment of a new school where youth could have its chance. In the young people he saw the only hope for awakening Denmark out of defeatism.

First there appeared a religious movement as a result of Grundtvig's opposition to rationalism and dead orthodoxy. The leaders of this movement were largely laymen. Grundtvig, a churchman, hesitated at first to approve of private religious gatherings; but he soon realized the power and possibilities of such activities. Although it cost him his ministerial office, he joined the movement.

---

[1] "Reply of the Church."

Three Visits to England.—From his three visits to England (1829, 1830, 1831) his idea of general enlightenment matured. He saw much good in England which he later brought to Denmark. He was impressed with the simple, free life of the average English family; the busy life of London taught him the blessing and necessity of work; he experienced the heroic spirit of the North; he admired the freedom of the English people.

His Opportunity.—When Grundtvig returned to Denmark in 1830 he found conditions favorable for his contribution. (The people wanted political freedom and the power to vote. To attain this freedom the common people should be enlightened and the means to this end was a folk high school where adults could be taught the history of Denmark from its beginning. They should also be taught the laws of their own and other countries. They should know well their own language so as to enable them to express themselves freely.)

N. F. S. Grundtvig

In 1838 Grundtvig expounded his ideas in a series of lectures in Copenhagen and later throughout the country. Students from the University, men and women of every occupation, came to hear him. He stood before them as the hero of the day, as the Liberator of Denmark. As the mature man of fifty-five he pleaded with his audiences to support his cause.

"Mands Minde."—In 51 lectures he expressed himself on many historical events in Denmark as well as in other countries. To Grundtvig youth is the time of vigor and of development. He calls on youth to in-

augurate a new period in Denmark's history. And this
they are to do with songs flowing from a heart that
loves God and country. In such love there is strength
and hope. Grundtvig pointed to a glorious past, filled
with heroic deeds and in the same breath he points to
a way in which this heroic past can be revived; namely,
through the Folk High School.

Soon others took up the fight for liberty and equality.
People's meetings for discussion of problems were held
throughout the country. Grundtvig's ideas and personal
philosophy gained followers everywhere and the movement for enlightenment had started before the first
Folkehøjskole at Rødding (1844) had even been established. At every meeting new leaders were won for
the schools that were to transform the Danish people.

The End of a Busy Life.—Grundtvig spent the rest
of his life working for the folk school, writing national
and religious songs, writing historical accounts, lecturing, preaching, and singing. He was a member of the
Danish Rigsdag (Congress). Grundtvig was married
three times, his first two wives preceding him in death.
He had several children, the youngest of which came to
America and inspired the idea of establishing folk high
schools.

Grundtvig was a great student and a versatile scholar.
He wrote about 20 volumes. It is said that for 30 years
he never slept a whole night in bed but had the habit
of dividing his sleep into three periods during the 24
hours. He enjoyed unusual health until his death on
September 2, 1872. He was active in the ministry until
he laid down life's task at the age of almost 90 years.
The hour he died he was working on a sermon for the
following Sunday.

The prophet of the North accomplished a great work
for his country, for into the Danish people Grundtvig

had put a national spirit which brought life, courage, vigor, and satisfaction to young and old. His work as a poet, historian, statesman, clergyman, and patriot will long be remembered; but his work as an educator and friend of youth is little known except in Northern Europe. Gradually his views on education are finding their way to other nations facing the same problems as Denmark did in the eighteenth century. To such nations the national and educational principles of Grundtvig have a message of great importance.

II. Kristen Kold

Through the night of doubt and sorrow
Onward goes the pilgrim band,
Singing songs of expectation,
Marching to the Promised Land.
Clear before us, through the darkness,
Gleams and burns the guiding light.
Brother clasps the hand of brother,
Stepping fearless through the night.

—B. S. Ingemann.

The Development of a Practical Man.—While Grundtvig supplied the philosophy and psychology for the People's College, the task of putting them into practice was left to a man who came from the common people. Kristen Kold, born in Thisted, Western Jutland, March 29, 1816, was the son of an industrious shoemaker.

The common school made little impression on the young Kold, but the stories his mother told of ancient people and heroes were never forgotten. Years after he related how his mother would gather the children of the neighborhood and, through stories, awaken interest in the past. Already then he experienced the power of the "living word," which could "speak to the heart, and make men kind, happy, and free."[1]

---

[1] Schrøder, p. 102.

At the age of eleven the question arose regarding his future work. His father wanted him to be a shoemaker, but soon found that the young Kold was not fit for that kind of work. This became his motto for life: "Where nothing is, nothing comes; where there is a little, there is room for God's blessing."

According to his mother's wish, young Kold entered a teachers' training school. At that time the teaching profession was not esteemed very highly in Denmark. Those who were not physically fit for regular work were often chosen to be school teachers.

His First School.—When Kold came to be introduced to his first school and saw the size of some of the boys he trembled. Most of them were his superior in physical strength. But when he was called upon to address the children in the presence of the parents he told them that he had not come to fight with them. He closed with these words: "You shall soon experience that I know more than you do; if you are wise, you will seek knowledge from me."[1]

When the parents heard this, they thought there was good sense in it. This first experience in speaking also showed the common sense which Kold possessed.

At the end of the school year Kold went to a large estate to be tutor for a period of three years. In his spare moments he would tell stories and recite comedies to the hired servants. Every one listened to him with interest.

In 1834 at the age of 18 he enrolled at Snedsted Teachers College. Here Kold met P. K. Algreen, a shoemaker's son who was teaching at the college. Algreen proved a life-long friend who often came to the assistance of Kold.

---

[1] Begtrup, "Det Danske Folks Historie," Vol. III, p. 243.

In the classroom Kold asked many questions and the teachers thought he was an ignoramus. But Kold informed the teachers that he was not satisfied with understanding half of what was said; he wanted to understand all of it.

An Important Question.—It was at this time that Kold faced the question: "Are you a Christian?" After much thought and prayer he experienced that a person is a Christian when he possesses and shows the love of God. Kold rejoiced in having this question satisfactorily solved.

In October of 1836, Kold was graduated and at once became tutor at a parsonage on Mors. Here Kold found many Christian friends who gathered occasionally for religious meetings. But considerable opposition arose in the press, and Kold sought another position, this time as teacher in a regular school. Again he began to hold meetings for young men and women but the school authorities asked him to leave at the end of the school year.

In Foreign Countries.—Thus Kold was faced by many trials until at last he decided to enter a mission in America. Since this did not materialize, Kold was asked to leave for Syria and Turkey with L. D. Hass who had decided to work among the Greek Christians. Rev. Hass wanted Kold to put his folk school ideas into practice among the Greeks. But first he was a servant for Rev. Hass and family. Kold was not anxious to go, yet he did consent to make the trip as he wanted to get away from Denmark.

After a year in Turkey, Kold left the home of Rev. Hass to do bookbinding. This was not very profitable and he experienced poverty and great hardship. After

five years at different kinds of work, he returned to
Denmark by way of Italy and walked across Europe.

As Kold many years later looked back upon his experiences, he felt that they were part of his training
for the work he was to do in Denmark.

Kold in the Army.—Shortly after Kold's return, the
War of 1848 broke out and he joined the army. "Until
then (referring to the spirit of the army) I had known
only how my own enthusiasm could be roused by some
great utterance and how I in turn could pass it on to
other individuals; but at this time I witnessed the inspiring of an entire people. For the first time I realized
what national spirit is."[1]

A New Experiment.

In 1849, Kold came to Ryslinge, Funen, to be tutor
for the children of Rev. V. Birkedal, an outstanding
Christian leader and preacher of the Grundtvigian persuasion. It was here that his ideas of a folk high school
found expression. Kold experimented with some children between the ages of 14 and 16. The first winter he
taught Bible history and Danish history, and the second
year, World history. Classes were conducted in the
parsonage. His spiritual presentation of history appealed to all; but Kold soon realized that his thoughts
were more for young men of the age of 20. Kold felt
that in the transition period, where the boy becomes
a young man, he needs guidance. On the other hand
Kold discovered that the boy of 15 did not sufficiently
understand nor appreciate moral and spiritual values.
This made Kold, the ardent realist and practical philos-
opher, turn his attention to a group of 20 young men
who worked on the nearby farms. These he gathered

---

[1] Begtrup, "Det Danske Folks Historie," Vol. III, p. 262.

every Saturday evening for discussions of historical subjects. In them Kold discovered a "total lack of the poetical spirit."[1] He also found that they enjoyed smoking their pipes, flirting with the girls, and in general were less easily moved by spiritual things.

The Development of a Folk School.—A group of interested farmers in Dalby and a new organization called "Oplysningsselskab" (Society for Enlightenment) started in Copenhagen for the specific purpose of building a folk high school, found in Christen Kold the man to make the new movement a success.

Algreen who was now in Copenhagen and an active member of the newly formed Society invited Kold to the capital. Kold accepted the invitation and together they called on Grundtvig. During the conversation the question of the age of students was discussed. Grundtvig said the students should be at least eighteen and have practical experience with ordinary problems in life. Kold, after raising some objections, said that through experiments he was inclined now to agree with him.

But how should Kold get money with which to build a new school? He had only 500 Rigsdaler ($250.00). But Grundtvig advised him to take a subscription list and ask his friends in Funen to give financial aid. Grundtvig was the first to sign the list with a contribution of 50 Rigsdaler ($25.00). With Grundtvig's name on the list, it was easy for Kold to raise funds for a new building. Neighbors did most of the work free of charge. In the fall of 1851, the new folk school, located northwest of Ryslinge, was dedicated. It was without debt and could accommodate about 20 boarding students. That same fall Kold sent out an official announcement.

---

[1] Begtrup, "Det Danske Folks Historie," Vol. III, p. 268.

KOLD'S FIRST ANNOUNCEMENT OF THE OPENING OF THE PEOPLE'S COLLEGE AT RYSLINGE IN 1851[1]

1. The school session will run from November first to April first.

2. Twenty pupils between the ages of fifteen and twenty will be accepted. Of these ten can be lodged in the school; the rest will be accommodated in the village and surrounding country. The tuition fee has been fixed at 20 kroner and the cost of food and lodging at 40 kroner.

3. Two teachers will be appointed if the Minister of Education will contribute to their salaries from the funds of the Sorø Academy.

4. The course has been arranged to occupy two winter sessions. Oral instruction will be given the first winter. The second will be devoted to written work. The pupils are to be divided into two classes of ten each.

5. The studies will comprise: (a) lecture on universal history outline broadly in which the historical atlas "Tiden's Strøm" will be used; (b) the Bible story will be told, in connection with which the student may read either Mueller's, Sørensen's, or Grundtvig's history of the Bible; (c) extracts from church history, especially our own sects and creeds; (d) the history of Denmark and Norse mythology will be told the pupils as a narrative and will then be studied in Oehlenschlæger's "The Norse Gods," with Mueller's "History of Denmark," Saxo and Snorre as supplementary reading; (e) geography in board outline and the use of the globe, with some description of the different countries and peoples, to be followed by Danish geography with some statistical references; (f) on the evenings devoted to entertainments, selected writings from Danish authors will be read, three successive weeks for each author; (g) singing with special reference to the old lays of the heroes. Finally, instruction in the usual school studies will be continued in a way to teach the student their practical use, where in most other schools these studies are simply memorized mechanically. The cost of tuition and maintenance for five months will amount to 60 kroner. While this charge is as low as it is possible to make it, it is higher than many people who would like to give their children a thorough education can afford. We have therefore arranged to distribute the payment over a number of years. For instance, a man who wishes to send his son at once need pay only 20 kroner the first and second winter and the remainder of the cost, if necessary, may be extended over the following

---

[1] Hollman, "The Folk High School," pp. 73-75.

five, ten, fifteen or twenty years. On the other hand, some other man whose son has not yet reached the required age may begin his yearly payments at once which will be placed to his credit, to be drawn upon later.

The school will open November first of the current year and payment will be required annually January first.

Very respectfully,

Ryslinge, June 1, 1851.   Kristen Kold.

When November arrived only one student had registered. Dismayed and disheartened Kold went into the near-by woods where he prayed fervently for students. When he returned he found 10 students and before the year was over the number had increased to 15. This brought satisfaction to Kold and his assistant, Poulsen Dal.

The Danish Cabinet, after considering an application for assistance, decided to give 100 Rigsdaler ($50.00). This sum was later increased to 400 Rigsdaler ($200.00). Despite opposition from various individuals and organizations to this aid, the cabinet continued to give its consent. This was a source of great encouragement to Kold and he was grateful for it.

Since practically all of the students were from Dalby, Kold moved his school to that place for the 1852-53 winter term. At Dalby, Kold taught in the common school (70 pupils) and in the folk school (20 students). This was almost too much for him, but he carried on his work for the sake of youth. And when a special delegation in 1858 came to inspect the school and found the work satisfactory, Kold had his reward.

Although his school at Dalby continued to grow, Kold desired to open a school closer to the new railway which had been built across Funen. A favorable site was bought at Dalum near Odense, the home of H. C. Andersen. Here he labored faithfully until his death, in 1870. He saw his new school increase in enrollment to about a hundred. This school is now the largest agricultural college in Denmark.

Many tributes have been given Kold in and outside of Denmark. The folk school leader, Ludvig Schrøder, from Askov, writes this about Kold: "Kold influenced the folk school movement so that the emphasis came to be on the awakening and enlightenment of personality more than it had been before his time. That so many young men and women come from the ranks of the common people was largely due to Kold. We thank him for this."[1]

Thornton, the English educator, has given Kold this significant estimate: "Kold was a sort of rustic blend of Socrates and Pestalozzi; he had a ready store of idiomatic Danish, had thought much about life and its problems, had a keen insight into human character, possessed an unlimited store of illustrations and experiences, and was consumed by a passion for communicating to others what had brought light and help to himself."[2]

The following remarks might serve as a fitting conclusion to this brief story of the life and character of Kristen Kold:

Kold was a great Christian personality with an unusual amount of common sense.

He was a practical educator, willing to change after the results of experiments taught him new methods more desirable.

He possessed considerable persistency which was combined with a strong faith in what he was doing.

His simple way of living and speaking has made the folk school a democratic institution.

---

[1] Schrøder, "Den Nordiske Folkehøjskole," p. 123.

[2] Quoted by Hegland, "The Danish People's High School, p. 92.

III. Grundtvig's Psychology of Education

Grundtvig left no book on the psychology of education. It is found in the context especially in "Mands Minde" and "Den Christelige Bornelærdom." The following paragraphs are therefore an interpretation, which, according to the writer's knowledge, is the first ever made in Danish or English of the principles of psychology which proved so successful in their application.

His Psychology Developed.—It is interesting to observe how Grundtvig arrived at his psychology of education. His method is unique in history and is closely related to his philosophy of life.

Grundtvig, from his study of the world and its history, arrived at the conclusion that this world which shows order, unity, and purpose, indicates also an eternal plan which only an Almighty God could have created. This conviction was further confirmed by a thorough study of the revelation of God in the Bible and in Jesus Christ. This led him to believe in the unity and essence of the Triune God—Father, Son, and Holy Spirit.

Grundtvig then turned to man. He reasoned that when God is one and the creation is one then man being a part of this creation and made in the image of God[1] must consequently consist of one indivisable personality —body and soul. Thus we observe that the unity of God led Grundtvig to the conviction of the unity of man.

Since all men have a common Father in God and men everywhere in any age are fundamentally alike, the concept of man must be a universal concept. The universality of man biologically, socially, and spiritually, makes it possible, Grundtvig believed, for universal principles to function in a variety of situations in all men.

---

[1] "The Holy Bible," Genesis 1:27.

Since God is one and the Creator of all things, His laws—spiritual, moral, and natural—are all universal. When man transgresses the laws of nature, he is punished by nature; if, however, he transgresses the spiritual and moral laws innate in the conscience,[1] which are universal, the conscience suffers. To Grundtvig this was universally true. To him the Ten Commandments contained universal truths of living and conduct showing a universal principle. While this was true of the Old Testament, it is so much more true of the New Testament which contains a universal religion that knows no boundaries. That Grundtvig should arrive at this conclusion seems natural as Christianity comprises his philosophy of life.

When man, then, is universal and possesses a unity in personality, it must be possible, yea, natural for him to think of principles in terms of wholes and applicable to a great variety of situations which may not be very closely related. And this is the beginning of Grundtvig's psychology of education. A person does not need a specific situation to be taught a specific principle. Such teaching Grundtvig did not believe was consistent with the unity of man.

To show how Grundtvig differed in his psychology of learning we need only refer to one prominent American psychologist, Thorndike, who writes:

> Training the mind means the development of thousands of particular independent capacities, the formation of countless particular habits, for the working of any mental capacity depends upon the concrete data with which it works. Improvement of any mental function or activity will improve others only in so far as they possess elements common to it also. The amount of identical elements in different mental functions and the amount of general influence from special training are much less than common opinion supposes.[2]

---

[1] "The Holy Bible," Romans 2:15.
[2] Thorndike, "Principles of Teaching," p. 248.

To Grundtvig the problem of transfer of training was fundamental for the development of personality. Grundtvig's aim was the development of personality through the teaching of universal principles. He felt that the brief time in which students generally would stay at a cultural institution would be too short for the teaching of specific habits. But he believed that numerous illustrations should be made of how the principle actually worked in specific situations. He also believed that practice of a principle was an important factor to be reckoned with, but he warns against overestimating the effect upon the individual.

The experiments by Bagley[1] tend to confirm Grundtvig's conviction of the transfer of learning. Bagley found in experimenting with some children that when they were taught to be neat with papers in arithmetic, the idea or principle of neatness did not transfer to English papers. After this discovery Bagley changed the experiment. Stories about neatness in general with numerous successful illustrations were told the children. The result of this experiment was that the children showed improvement of neatness in general. In other words, the child had learned the principle or idea of neatness. The habit was no longer attached to papers in arithmetic, although it would be applicable in that subject also. Bagley drew the conclusion that transfer of training takes place outside of specific situations and that principles do function in a variety of new situations. This experiment confirms Grundtvig's contention of a century ago.

It was Grundtvig's psychology of learning which became the basic method of teaching in the People's Colleges. The entire system of education is built on the assumption that transfer of training takes place in a

---

[1] Bagley, "The Educative Process," pp. 203-217.

variety of situations after a principle has been established. For example, the students at these institutions are not encouraged to do much reading, but they are encouraged to be intellectually alert to new ideas and things. The remarkable result has been that the Danish people constitute a nation of readers. There is hardly a rural home without a library and at least one daily newspaper and several farm magazines. Practically every rural community has its own established library. The reason for this situation can be traced to the People's Colleges.

Grundtvig's Psychology of Learning Applied.—When Grundtvig had thus developed his psychology of learning, he began to consider ways and means to establish a new cultural institution where youth could have its chance. The opportunity soon arrived. With the fall of Napoleon in 1814, Denmark was left a disheartened people and a country ruined economically. This situation challenged the powers of Grundtvig. He heard the prophetic words, "Comfort ye, comfort ye my people, saith the Lord." Thus with a feeling of holy duty and a deep love for the common people, Grundtvig was able to render his great and lasting service to his nation.

His Christian principles made him thoroughly democratic. Truly could he sing:

> And be we poor and lowly
> Yet are we sons of kings
> And higher than the eagle
> Hope may spread out her wings.

Grundtvig's main interest was in the enlightenment of the common people, especially the people of the rural communities. He believed in the nobility of man and in the fact that man is the crown of all God's cre-

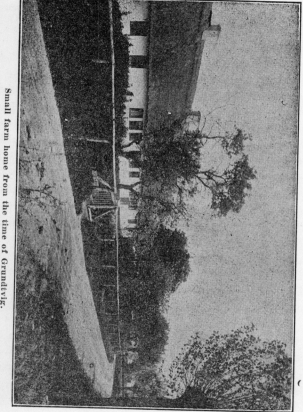

Small farm home from the time of Grundtvig.

ation.[1] In the spirit of this high conception of man and in simple language, he tried to bring the great thoughts of the ages to the people. How well the following conception by Carlyle applies to Grundtvig:

> The subject of education is man. And who and what is man? He is not a worm of dust, nor is he a butterfly of beautiful existence; rather he is the child of God, a creature born into an infinite universe and destined for an eternal existence.[2]

Grundtvig taught his countrymen to sing even while at work; he taught them to appreciate the beauty and joy in good literature; he taught them to appreciate their own country through the study of history. He believed that the ideals and spirit of a nation are expressed in its history and literature, and that a people could be awakened only through a realization of them. This thought has found a place in the People's College where the subjects are taught from a historical point of view.

The real reason for the work which Grundtvig did for the enlightenment of the Danish people is found in his deep love for humanity and for his country, ennobled as he was by a strong Christian faith. This feeling is shown in his kindness toward the common people. Like Carlyle, he had respect for the common sense of the farmer and the rough hands of the laborer. The upper classes of society ought never to forget the root from which they sprang, nor their origin from, and dependence upon the common worker. Grundtvig's love for the masses was not the kind that wished to change the historical development of the workers. He saw no humiliation in being a tiller of the soil, or a common laborer; nor did he see any glory in riches or abstract knowledge. To Grundtvig, disaster was connected with ignorance, immorality, and godlessness. In

---

[1] "The Holy Bible," Genesis 1:28-30; Psalms 8:5, 6.
[2] Thwing, "Education," p. 39.

one of his numerous songs he points to what he considers the highest personal value: "To know God and oneself."

In the above sentence lies the very foundation for the People's College. To know God and oneself is true cultural education. Such an education is not scientific in the strict sense of that word, for scientific education is technical, and can hardly become the possession of the masses. Most individuals may be able to gather a few fragments of scientific knowledge; but such knowledge is "childish," utters Grundtvig, and has little, if any, scientific value, and very little cultural value.

From the Jews, Grundtvig learned that education must be religious; from the Greeks, political. Roman history taught him to guard against knowledge and physical power that act apart from conscience and heart.

In a series of polemical discourses, he criticized the old system of education, which he believed had come from the Romans, and the mistaken idea that knowledge without integration, and intellectual attainment without development of personality, are able to ennoble the individual and bring to him a greater satisfaction. From this false conception, Grundtvig wished to save the common people. Furthermore, he did not wish to let the common people receive scientific knowledge from books before they, through the "living word," had been orientated in the world of general knowledge. Book-learning, without the individual's ability to judge intelligently, is dangerous, and may cause idle dreaming and dissatisfaction with the humble and ordinary calling of manual work. Education must not be of such a nature that it causes the individual to underestimate the value of unskilled labor, but should, instead, tend to increase the desire and ability to do ordinary work well. Therefore, education must not merely be scientific nor of the textbook type, but of the kind which preserves a balance between understanding the universe and understanding the individual. Education must be a preparation for life; education **is** life.

It is natural that every form of enlightenment, including that of the masses, must utilize science and literature in their widest sense, but these must be only one of several means used to develop the power of judgment and spiritual independence. If **enlightenment** is to be of real value, and bring worthy fruit, it must **influence the whole personality from within.** Such an enlightenment awakens the conscience, strengthens morality, and develops responsibility. Only when this has been accomplished, can an individual be said to have a cultural education. This education may be acquired by the masses.

Thus Grundtvig laid the foundation for the People's College. What Pestalozzi had been to children, Grundtvig now became to youth.

IV. Early Beginnings of the Folkehøjskole Movement

Grundtvig's plan of establishing a large People's College at Sorø, which would serve as a cultural center for the nation came to naught when King Christian VIII died in 1848. Despite this unfortunate event his ideas found development in another way and in another place.

North Schleswig favored a Danish nationalizing movement. This movement led to the organization of the Schleswig Association which founded a People's College at Rødding. In the application to the King for opening this school the purpose is clearly stated in the following excerpt by Schrøder:

> The aim we have set before us is to be found in an institution where peasant and citizen may acquire such knowledge and accomplishments as may minister to his

usefulness and enjoyment, with reference not so much
to his particular vocation and work as to his function
as his country's son and citizen of the State. The institution should have, therefore, a beneficent influence upon
his private and home life, as well as upon his public and
civic activity. We call it a high school because it is not
to be an ordinary boys' school, but an educational institution partly for young men past the age of confirmation
(fourteen or fifteen years of age) and partly for full-
grown boys and men. We call it a people's high school
because persons of every station may attend it, even if
it is especially arranged for the rural class and expects
its students from that source.[1]

The Rødding People's College began instruction in
November, 1844, with twenty students and two teachers. John Wegener, a university graduate, became its
first principal.

When the minister of education tried to introduce
examinations the new principal, Professor Høgsbro, re-
plied:

The aim of the school is to awaken and nourish appreciation for the life of the spirit. Especially is it concerned
with increasing love of country by giving information a-
bout its language and literature, nature, and history, its
conditions in the past and present. In addition, however,
it does not lay less stress on giving students love for and
knowledge of agriculture.[2]

The fulfillment of such an aim would be hindered if
the subjects were to be taught and received with an
examination. Høgsbro continues:

This institution has no desire to underestimate the
importance of technical knowledge nor the developing
of a clear and incisive mind. Its aim, however, is essentially to educate for practical living. We deem the development of the will and the emotions more important
than the exercising of the memory and the intellect.
The aim is to achieve in secular matters what the church
does in the religious field. It is of far greater significance to our school to have succeeded in arousing a feeling for what is high and noble among the students and
to have stimulated the accomplishment of great ends
than to have taught them any facts or to have them understand a new definition in grammar or the solving of

---

[1] Quoted by Schrøder, "Den Denske Folkehøjskole," p. 46.
[2] Quoted by Hegland, "The Danish People's High School," p. 87.

a mathematical problem. Such things are a part of school work but merely supplementary to the other aim. Instruction is to be an aid to living rather than to learning. We desire that our pupils should leave filled with enthusiasm to devote themselves to the problems of life and with some understanding of the opportunities which life offers. What they lack in knowledge may be easily acquired and their intelligence will develop in the course of their work.[1]

After the disastrous war of 1864-1866 in which Denmark lost Schleswig to Germany, a new school was founded under the able and eminent leadership of the teacher and historian, Ludvig Schrøder. This institution, located at Askov in Southern Jutland, was destined to become a great cultural center.

Although the school at Rødding was founded before Kold came to Ryslinge, it was Kold's school which became the model for future folk schools. The success of his work appealed to many educators so that from 1860 to 1870 there was a surprising increase in folk schools, as the following table shows:

Period	People's Colleges	Agricultural Colleges
1844-1850	2	4
1851-1860	11	5
1861-1870	50	7
1871-1880	64	10
1881-1890	67	13
1891-1900	74	11
1901-1910	83	19
1911-1920	65	21
1921-1925	64	22
1926-1930	59	22
1931-1937	59	21

The reduction in number of schools was caused by the World War, financial difficulties, and the desire on the part of some to unite with larger schools. In that same period, student attendance rose from 7869 to 9726. It was realized by some educators that the opportunities would be greater if there were several teachers, rather than two, as was the case in some schools.

---

[1] Quoted by Hollman, "The Folk High School," pp. 58-59.

The following figures show the attendance at People's Colleges since 1844. The year is counted from April 1 to March 31:

	Men	Women	Total
1844-45	46		46
1854-55	227	40	267
1864-65	295	31	326
1874-75	2420	1131	3551
1884-85	2760	1472	4232
1894-95	3261	2469	5730
1904-05	4371	3302	7673
1914-15	3539	3291	6830
1924-25	5727	3992	9719
1934-35	5835	3531	9366

If Grundtvig and Kold knew of the success their schools have had they would rejoice; the young men and women who have benefited and will benefit are their reward.

The Danish People's Colleges have been visited by people from all over the world. They have been studied from many points of view as the following estimates will verify.

Einar Jensen, Principal Agricultural Economist for the United States Department of Agriculture, looks at the People's College from an economic point of view. He says:

> This school movement has been a powerful factor in making Denmark a most democratic country, and caused democracy to grow with industrial production in contrast to other countries where it often wanes with pioneer life. Without these schools it is hardly thinkable that the farmers, although they had the political power together with the Social Democrats, could carry through a social legislation which is now considered the model for industrialized countries. It is also interesting to note that of the present government which has been formed by the Labor Party, which in Denmark calls itself the Social Democrats, half the ministers have, at one time, attended a folk school.[1]

Th. Madsen Mygdal, formerly Prime Minister of Denmark, says: "The indirect influence of the work of the

---

[1] Jensen, "Danish Agriculture," p. 102.

People's Colleges is traced most strongly and clearly in the development of agriculture. The reason is that farm youth attend the People's College and thereby benefit by its instructions."[2]

Sir Michael Sadler, Master of University College, Oxford, speaks these significant words about the contribution, the People's College:

> A little sentimental perhaps to our ears, but sincere and, as events proved, in the highest degree practical. The People's High Schools founded by Grundtvig and his disciples (chief among them Christian Kold 1816-1870) gave the essence of a liberal education to farmers' sons and daughters. The humanities, which was all that the schools taught, did not breed ineffectuals. Between 1860 and 1880 they worked a miracle of culture in the Danish country side. The town folk were, as a whole, impervious. But the peasantry was transformed.[3]

[2] "Den Danske Folkehøjskole," p. 137.
[3] Begtrup, "The Folk High Schools of Denmark," p. 9.

CHAPTER III

THE PEOPLE'S COLLEGE

I am just a simple farmer
Downright and plain,
And yet I love my modest calling,
For around my little home
Grow blossoms fair
With color and perfume.
Mine is the clear spring,
Mine is the fresh breeze.

I grow up to the song of the birds,
Learned a little of them too.
I sing when the impulse comes
To fly light and free.
I sing behind the plough
And to the sound of the mowing.
Hills and woods
Give back my song.

And when I am weary with toil
And day is done,
My spirit is fresh, my mind at ease,
I am happy and free.
I would not change places
With any man on earth
Nor will I leave this spot in the North.

—Mads Hansen.

The Meaning of "Folkehøjskole."—The Danish "Folkehøjskole," as founded by Grundtvig and Kold, has a
meaning which a literal translation—"folk high school"
—does not properly convey. The English equivalent,
"high school," suggests a school for adolescents. "Folkehøjskole" in Denmark is a school for adults of eighteen years of age or over.

If one is to understand the Danish institutions, it becomes necessary to forget the American academic nomenclatures and traditions. American high school education is thought of in terms of the acquisition of a certain number of credits. This holds true to about the same extent in college training. The number of credits determines the place of a student—freshman, sophomore, junior, or senior. Thus, according to our academic traditions, the Danish pupil would belong to the class designated by the American school system as the freshman class since he enters these folk high schools with an eighth grade diploma.

But, may we conjecture, are credits alone the most intelligent method of rating the intellectual ability of youth? A certain number of credits does not necessarily represent a certain quantity of knowledge, or its quality either. Yet, we have accepted credits as the most favorable method of rating. The result has been a conditioned progress—that is, a progress conditioned by credits.

The truest test of intelligence, it seems to the writer, is a person's ability to think independently. Often the many systematically developed and logical courses in American education leave little opportunity for thinking. In a number of instances the writer of the textbook and the instructor do most of the thinking for the student. Outside of class, the student, thus nurtured, has little if any time for actual thinking. Unlike the Danish student, who devotes four years or more to practical work that requires initiative and planning before entering college, the American student continues school twelve, and even sixteen years, without interruption. It is the writer's contention that such long periods of traditional college application leave little time for the best thinking and less opportunity for discovering the student's own powers and possibilities.

The average Danish student has a sense of personal and social responsibility which is unique. The four years of manual work teaches him this valuable lesson. On coming to the People's College these students do not study because they have to, nor because they expect a substantial, material return for their efforts. There are no examinations, for example; no grade marks; and no degrees. Those students must have other stimuli as incentives for study. What these young people want is to enrich and develop further the everyday life they lived before coming to the People's College. It is undoubtedly such an education that Newman refers to when he says:

> We speak of the communication of knowledge as being Education. We thereby really imply that that knowledge is a state or condition of mind; and since cultivation of mind is surely worth seeking for its own sake, we are thus brought once more to the conclusion, which the word "liberal" and the word "philosophy" have already suggested: That there is a knowledge which is desirable, though nothing comes of it, as being of itself a treasure, and a sufficient remuneration of years of labour.[1]

Unlike the average American student incentives, there are few objectives, or better objective forces, to spur the Danish student toward intellectual attainment. What he wants to find is a solution to the problems which have arisen during his four years of contact with real life as it unfolded itself to him in daily work and during his leisure hours. A student with such a desire is truly of college rank. It seems proper, then, to designate these institutions as "People's Colleges."

Location.—In order to exert the proper influence upon the farm community and create a favorable environment for the students, the eighty Danish People's Col-

---

[1] Newman, "University Education," p. 114.

leges and Agricultural Schools are all located in rural communities, except the college at Lyngby. This is an important factor when we consider the sources from which the students come. Of all students, sixty-five per cent come from the farm and the remaining thirty-five per cent from the rural labor class. The most remarkable fact is that ninety-eight per cent of these students return to their former occupations. In other words, out of 9000 students, only 180 change occupation after having attended the People's College. This shows then that these schools have not educated youth away from manual work but rather educated them to do their work better.

Administration.—The colleges are owned by various groups. Of the fifty-nine People's Colleges which were operating in 1936, seventeen were owned by college associations, thirty by directors, and twelve by private individuals. Of the twenty-one agricultural colleges, eight were owned by directors, while five were owned by private parties.[1] In any case, the director, whether he owns the institution or is merely elected, has full control in the matter of administration and curriculum.

There are five sources of income for the colleges. These are the college associations, the college farm, student fees, the county, and the state. During the year 1935-36, the counties gave aid to the extent of about $10,000, while the state contributed $160,000, besides the aid given to needy students.[2] State and county contributions are given to the institutions without specifying how or where thee funds are to be spent.

Although many of the schools have old buildings,

---

[1] "Folkehøjskoler of Landbrugsskoler samt Husholdningsskoler," 1937, p. 7.
[2] "Ibid.," p. 10.

they are well kept and well equipped with laboratories, library, gymnasium, and steam heated rooms. A beautiful garden or park usually surrounds the building. A college farm gives access to agricultural experiments and observations. This farm generally has the latest in machinery and pure bred livestock, and continually carries on experiments in crop raising.

The schools are boarding schools with all of the students living in the dormitory. Often the director and some of the teachers have special apartments in the main building. Once each day teachers and students share a simple but substantial and nourishing meal together. This has a wholesome effect upon the students who are inclined to be democratic in spirit.

In harmony with the philosophy of the institutions, the furnishings in the lecture rooms and dormitory are very simple. Most of the students come from simple homes and return to simple homes. Few alterations in standards of living are therefore necessary, nor do the students have to spend much time in orientating themselves. They have few adjustments to make when coming to the institution and less to make when returning to their former occupation. The People's College believes in "plain living and high thinking."

The Teachers.—The underlying principle in the activities of the People's College, as Grundtvig conceived it, is that **all influence must be personal.** The success of this depends on **how** the information is presented, or even more on **who** gives it. The first condition for teaching in these schools is that the teacher, besides being well informed and having pedagogical ability, must himself enjoy his calling and possess a power and burning zeal in his personality and word, that can hold the attention of his hearers. If the eyes and ears of youth are to be opened, if the power and will of youth are to be tested and developed, then it must first of all be evident in the personality of the teacher, for only then can the teacher impress the students.

The Danes soon realized that if the teacher is to accomplish such a great task he must be satisfied with life. Therefore each college provides comfortable homes with gardens or furnished apartments in the main building of the institution. With a salary varying from 2500 Kroner to 4000 Kroner[1] the teacher and his family can live comfortably year after year in the same place. Most of the teachers retain the same position at least ten years and a considerable number teach a life-time in the same institution.

Although the primary qualification for teaching in the People's College is one of character and personality, more than one-third of the teachers have academic training, holding, for the most part, the bachelor of arts degree or its equivalent. Many possess the master of arts degree, and not a few hold a doctor of philosophy degree. The majority of the teachers are graduates from teacher-training schools. They have chosen teaching, not as a stepping stone to something else, but as a life profession, giving their entire time and energy for the betterment of youth. They are practical idealists.

The important question which these teachers face is not how many facts they are able to present to the students but rather: Has youth through their teaching become receptive to the knowledge of life? If the teacher during the few months of school succeeds in awakening the mind of youth, then he will seek for himself the knowledge that he needs for his occupation. His eyes and ears will have been opened to the lessons of other men, and books will be his companions. If, however, this educational awakening in the youthful mind fails,

---

[1] One Danish Krone is equivalent to about twenty-two cents.

then factual and even cultural knowledge is of little avail because it has not become a part of him and it is doubtful that he will know how to apply it.

The Students.—The students coming to the People's College represent every sort of home and size of farm. Most of them have worked four years or more in order to attend school. As a rule they are strong, able-bodied young men and women between the ages of 18 and 25. Their contact with real life and hard work has taught them seriousness of purpose and the art of patience. They spend little time on thinking what their task "might have been," but rather what it is and how it can be improved.

These practical realists are taught to see the **ideal** behind the hard tasks of every-day life, to sing behind the plough under God's open sky, to feel the romance in working with nature, and to experience that it is good to live.

In view of these facts it is not difficult to understand that some of the best talents in Denmark have devoted their time to the future leaders of the nation. To be a sincere teacher of youth in Denmark is to be a great patriot.

These students, realizing their responsibility, are a discipline unto themselves in and out of the classroom. They punish any offender against the teachers, fellow students, and rules of the institution. It happens seldom that a student is removed from school for misbehavior. The students who come to these schools are interested in improving themselves and in getting something out of their precious time. They realize that the year at school is their golden opportunity in life.

During the year 1935-36 no less than 8,972 students attended People's Colleges and agricultural schools. The governmental aid to needy students amounted to about

$110,000. The aid given to each of the 3,867 students whose applications were accepted amounted to $45 for the year.[1] Since the monthly cost for room, board, and tuition for each student is about $18 the governmental assistance for a period of five months seems considerable as $45 would cover expenses for half the school term.

The Curriculum.—Since the students in general have few means and the school term is short, which subjects should be taught and how much time should be devoted to each? Grundtvig recommended Danish, history and literature. The curriculum has developed since the first institution was organized in 1844, as the list of courses below will show. The Statistical Department for the Bureau of Education in Denmark has averaged the number of hours devoted to each course in the People's Colleges of Denmark. The following averages are from the five-months' course for men:[2]

Courses	Number of Hours Devoted To Each Course
Danish	155
Handwriting	10
Reading	43
History	169
Sociology	16
Common Law	24
Geography	35
Physics	21
Chemistry	8
Zoology and Botany	15
Hygiene	19
Mathematics	108
Drawing	44
Music (Singing)	35
Gymnastics	103
Surveying	10
Bookkeeping (Agricultural)	27
Agricultural subjects	95
Other subjects	125

---

[1] "Folkehøjskoler of Landbrugsskoler samt Husholdningsskoler," 1937, p. 20.

[2] "Ibid.," p. 24.

Askov Folkehøjskole

This list of courses shows the amount of time devoted to Danish language and literature. Grundtvig considered the ability to express oneself clearly and fluently essential to an enlightened individual. As expected, history receives the most attention. This subject includes the political, social, and philosophical history of Denmark and the world. The social and natural sciences receive about equal attention. Mathematics includes the historical and practical aspects. Gymnastics, which continues later in community education, is a means of using surplus energy. Many of the students return to their respective communities to become leaders in gymnastic unions.

Such subjects as common law, chemistry, drawing, surveying, and bookkeeping are generally practical courses. The agricultural subjects deal with crop raising and stock breeding. Under the item of Other Subjects are found lectures of human interest, free discussions, and English or German. The student may take any or all of the subjects.

The following schedule from the two-year "Enlarged Co-Educational Inner Mission People's College" at Haslev, Zealand, during the winter term of 1937-1938, shows the variety and the apparently advanced subjects taught in order to give cultural education:

> Danish: 5 to 6 hours weekly. Dictation, analysis, recitation, theme writing on various subjects of human interest.
>
> Literature: 2 hours weekly. Study of poets and their literary works.
>
> Mathematics: 3 to 4 hours weekly. The historical and fundamental aspect of mathematics.
>
> Geography: 1 hour weekly.
>
> History: 2 hours weekly. Various periods in world history, with lectures on the sociological aspect.
>
> Church History: 2 hours weekly. Lectures on the deciding factors in the history of the church.
>
> History of Missions: 2 hours weekly. The motive, goal, and means of missions.
>
> Christian Theology: 1 to 2 hours weekly. A presentation of the fundamentals of Christianity.
>
> Psychology and Psychiatry: 2 hours weekly.
>
> Bible: 5 hours weekly. Old and New Testament.
>
> Open Forum: 1 hour weekly. All students. Aspects of everyday life considered and discussed.
>
> Bookkeeping: 1 hour weekly.
>
> English: 5 hours weekly. For beginners and advanced students.
>
> Gymnastics: 2 to 3 hours weekly. Physical education for all.
>
> Hygiene and Health Education: 1 hour weekly.
>
> Debate: Several hours weekly for those who wish it.
>
> The Question Period: 1 hour weekly.
>
> Special Courses for Women:
>
> Hand Work: 4 to 6 hours weekly.
>
> Samariter-Course: 2 hours weekly. Fundamentals of first aid and nursing.

Besides lectures by the regular staff members, outside speakers give instruction in special subjects.[1]

---

[1] Haslev People's College, Haslev, Zealand, "Bulletin of 1937-1938."

The Historical Method of Teaching.—History, which is studied for its own sake, is the main subject in the People's Colleges. How history is studied is difficult to explain as that largely depends upon the individual teacher. However, the general purpose found everywhere is to study outstanding **historical personalities** or let the lives of great presonalities throw light upon the lives of youth and the times. Of the two, the latter appears to be the more important. Lectures are also given on topics dealing with the relationship between men and women, parents and children, employer and employee, as well as with the religious, political, and social questions of the day and their historical background. Such lectures, followed by a general discussion, lead to a practical philosophy of life.

This spirited method of presenting historical facts, Grundtvig possessed to a maximum extent. Every history teacher of youth ought to use more of this life-like method of presentation. Out of historical data and events the instructor should bring a total, integrated whole, for only in so doing, can he understand their real value to our many-sided modern life.

The following excerpt shows how the historical method of teaching is employed in other subjects than history. Professor Paul LaCour, one of the most successful teachers to use Grundtvig's historical method, tells how he teaches a lesson in geometry:

> First I prepare the way for geometry by discussing the problems with which the ancients, notably the Egyptians, were confronted; attention is then directed to the beginnings of land surveys and the calculating of areas. In the ruins of Edfu we find evidence that the Egyptians calculated the superficial area of a quadrilateral by multiplying the mean length of the opposite sides by the mean length of the other two sides. It is easy to show the pupils that this method was not exact and that the work was done mechanically.
>
> We then proceed to the advances made by the Greeks, or speaking more accurately, we observe how Thales

went to Egypt and there became acquainted with all the great achievements in building. He afterwards returned to Miletus and founded the Ionic school; despite his wide knowledge of actual building operations, he nevertheless appreciated the great significance of theory. Legend tells us that on discovering the theorem, "The base angles of an isosceles triangle are equal," he sacrificed an ox to the gods. Why was there such a "to-do" about this theorem? Anybody able to measure with his eyes can surely see that if two beams of equal length are inclined on a horizontal plane against each other, the angles which they form with the base will be equal. There is certainly nothing important or interesting about this experiment. But Thales' genius was shown in his appreciating that it was a truth of general application.

It is well known that pupils, otherwise very talented, often find it difficult to get started in mathematics. Sometimes even after six months or more the student has not really understood anything, although he gets along by memorizing and hard work. He understands each separate theorem partially but does not take in the subject as a whole. It is perceived only dimly. Suddenly, somehow, the thing dawns upon him. After that, it all seems so incredibly easy that it is hard for him as well as the teacher, to understand why the subject should be hard for anybody. To have this realization come partly by chance seems to me pedagogically wrong. Since Thales' simple theorems can create, as we have seen, so great an impression when they are presented in their historic background, and enable the student to start easily, that is reason for beginning in this way.

Even if by these means the students have learned something of theory, in addition greater familiarity is desirable. I therefore continue the historical record, telling for instance of the difficulties when Anaximander and Anaximenes departed from Thales' method. Pythagoras followed Thales' way and made possible the solving of many problems which had been beyond the compass of ordinary men.

I then pass to the story of the Sophists' attack on mathematics. The well-known sophism of Achilles and the tortoise illustrates how a proposition obviously absurd may apparently be supported by mathematical demonstration. I point out the fallacy and how these attacks led mathematicians to greater care in stating their propositions so as to render them unassailable.

The realm of exact science is approached. Plato's analytic thoroughness is studied and enjoyed, and our course closes with Euclid unsurpassed with systematic presentation. His work really corresponds to Greek excellence in other realms of form, viz: architecture and the plastic arts.

Ollerup Folkehøjskole

Geometry is obviously that branch of mathematics which from the start was largely expressed in formulae. If I have succeeded in applying the historic method to geometry, it is of course much easier to do in other branches of mathematics.[1]

It is quite evident that the historical method so successfully employed by Professor LaCour can be taught only by the use of the spoken word in lectures. The students do not have the vocabulary nor the academic training necessary to understand advanced fields of thought in books. But in the lecture the teacher deals with great things in simple, everyday language. As a rule the teacher uses no textbooks or even notes in the lecture hall, nor do the students have textbooks in class or take many notes on the lecture. The taking of notes interferes with the teacher's free method of lecturing, and also tends to interrupt the trend of thought and the attention of the students. By having the eyes

[1] Quoted by Holman, "The Folk High Schools," pp. 128-131.

of the students centered on the teacher, the inspiration is mutual and the teacher can make necessary adjustments to meet the needs of the students. This method of teaching has been found favorable for the type of students attending and for the type of material presented.

Success Depending on Student Cooperation.—The People's College does not prepare students for higher institutions of learning; consequently, at the end of the school year there are no examinations. There seems to be a general understanding among the educators that such requirements, which examinations tend to impose upon teachers and students, would destroy the free and fruitful method of delivering and receiving the lectures. The value of attending these schools cannot be measured statistically or in dollars and cents. The purpose of the instruction is to develop the **"inner man,"** which all instruction ought to attempt to do.

Thomas Hughes in "Tom Brown's Schooldays" asks the question: "Why do I send my boy to school?" To which he answers: "If he can only be a courageous, useful, and truth-loving Englishman, a gentleman, and a Christian—that is all I wish!" The man who answered this question could well understand the underlying ideas of the Danish People's College, and he would rejoice in knowing that such schools now exist in many countries. He would also rejoice in reading the following letter written by a former student, a young woman whose words ring with joy and gratitude to the teachers who so faithfully and intelligently helped her to appreciate life. She writes in part:

> Youth is a period of unfolding in which longings are born and battles fought. It is often difficult to understand clearly the many new impressions and questions which force themselves upon us; nor is it easy to see one's own position in life. It is in such situations that the People's College is of inestimable help to many.
> We who have had the privilege and experience of

spending a few months of our youth at a People's College will undoubtedly agree that the time was indeed well spent.

It was a happy realization of a long felt desire when I came to Tommerup Hojskole. The kind reception, the friendly hand clasp, and the hearty "Velkommen," made me feel at home the very first evening I was there. I decided to use the coming days in this place in the most profitable way. We all felt that a new period which had, or would have lasting significance, had begun in our lives.

In truth, those were precious days. Light was shed upon many questions, our horizon of life was widened, and we saw greater and more opportunities in life than we had formerly anticipated.

We were given an impulse to strive for everything that is good and noble, and in reality worthy of our honest efforts. We learned to view the minutes as a gift from God, our work as a good companion, and our home as the dearest place on earth. Through motion pictures, lectures, and not least, the delightful excursions to places of natural beauty and historic importance we learned to appreciate and love our country.

The teacher pointed to opportunities that we should utilize. We were admonished to improve ourselves in our daily task so as to better fill our place in the world. As we walked through the woods, the withered branches and leaves noisily breaking underneath our feet, our eyes were opened by the botanist to appreciate the beauty and greatness of nature and we felt that life was joyful and rich, and that it was wonderful to live.

. . . It was with considerable regret that we parted with the teachers, the companions, and the places so rich in memory. We gave thanks to God for His kindness toward us during the many happy hours that we as teachers and students had had together. Thus, with enriched and renewed lives, we left for the tasks that awaited us.[1]

This letter is a splendid tribute to the institution founded by Grundtvig and Kold. Each year thousands of students leave these schools after having been awakened to an intelligent appreciation of life. Through the instruction and daily life with teachers and comrades, life values receive a new meaning and interpretation, and become an impetus for new attainments.

---

[1] Translated by the author from "Tommerup Højskole" by Forstander P. Sandback, 1934.

CHAPTER IV

CONTRIBUTION OF THE PEOPLE'S COLLEGE

I. COMMUNITY EDUCATION

Man was born for two things—thinking and acting.
—Cicero.

A New Educational Contribution.—After several years of absence the writer returned to Denmark during the winter of 1936-1937 to make a firsthand investigation of the People's Colleges and their contributions to the life and activity of the people. This investigation brought him in contact with individuals who had been at the People's Colleges within the last fifty years. These individuals belonged to practically every occupation, a large percentage of them being leaders in agriculture, government, cooperatives, community education, youth movement, and other important movements of the community. It brought him in contact with lecturing societies, gymnastic societies, and target-practice societies and other organizations that have been founded by former People's College students. The following pages are, therefore, largely a description of conditions as the writer found them.

In the two previous chapters the discussion centered around the founders, the foundings, and the functioning of a cultural college, known to the Danes as Folkehøj-skole and to the world as the People's College. The growth of this school was pointed out as being rather remarkable considering that they, in every instance, were undertaken by private individuals or associations. It is also remarkable when the size of Denmark is considered. This small country of 16,570 square miles, or about one-fourth of the size of North Dakota, has one cultural school for every 207 square miles. In other words, if the state of North Dakota were to have institutions according to this scale, it would mean about 833 cultural schools for adults for the 70,837 square miles. Since the farm population of Denmark is about one million there is one school to every 12,500 persons. In the case of North Dakota where the farm population is about 400,000 it would mean one school to every 1,201 persons. But many factors, such as variation in density of population and condition of soil, enter into this comparison which in a way makes it more artificial than real. The Danish institutions, which thus reach practically every part of Denmark, have exerted a great influence since no less than thirty-five per cent of the present rural population have attended these schools, another thirty-five per cent have come in contact with them through special college functions and activities, such as banquets, lectures, crop and breeding exhibitions, and the remaining thirty per cent in indirect contact through former students and local alumni organizations of which there is one in almost every community.

We, in America, are interested in knowing how the People's College operates, its administration and curriculum, teaching facilities and methods, and student life. But what we are even more interested in knowing is the direct or indirect influence, if any, which these schools have had upon the life and activities of the people. If there have been no distinct contributions by this system of education, there would be little value in considering it. And even if this system of education has made some contributions to the people of Denmark, are those contributions of such a nature that they would warrant the adoption of such a system of education in our country? This question the writer shall attempt to answer with real examples and from personal experience and observations in Denmark.

In order to awaken his countrymen to self-realization of their power and responsibility, Grundtvig travelled from one community to another lecturing on history and literature. Grundtvig was in favor of a complete national revival in spirit which included political, social, economic, and agricultural reform. The aristocracy had been in power for centuries. The tiller of the soil had been a servant of landlords. However, in 1849 a **constitution** was given to the people which provided equal representation in the upper and lower houses of parliament. This was an important step. But the rural population was not ready to resume its share of responsibility, consequently the wealthy land owners and members of the nobility continued to rule the nation. It took the disastrous war of 1864-66 with Austria and Germany, in which Denmark lost Schleswig-Holstein and part of southern Jutland, to prove the inability to maintain peace and understanding with other nations.

As a result of this great loss numerous People's Colleges were founded to revive the nation; and by 1875 about thirty-five per cent of the members of Parliament were former students of the new national institutions for enlightenment. The words of the founders designating the new movement as **"enlightened"** and **"enlivened"** were being fulfilled. A series of laws favorable to the farmer and common labor were passed due to the men thus inspired. Even Grundtvig became a member of the lower house (Folketinget) and later a member of the upper house (Landstinget) in order to wield his influence. Soon this new spirit made itself felt. Grundtvig and his associates in Parliament and his supporters were conservative in their measures and constructive in their criticisms. It is said of them that they never criticized without having, what they believed, a real substitute or remedy. The people soon rallied to support them with their votes and in the space of a decade the land owners and members of the nobility lost their prestige and power. Today, class distinction in Denmark is not one of blood, but rather one of wealth.

After the death of Grundtvig in 1872, in whose funeral procession were 200,000 mourners, the enlightened rural population carried on the fight for more liberal laws that would benefit the small land owner. It was in this period that cooperatives, of which we shall speak later, began to flourish. The one law of interest to every adult was that dealing with **common suffrage.** This finally became a reality in 1915. This was, in the opinion of the former students of the People's Colleges, an important part of the life of a nation. An enlightened people must be a responsible people, and vice versa. Therefore, the **political efforts** of the rural population did not end with the privilege to vote, for in 1919 a bill was introduced and passed which called for dissolution of a number of large estates into small farms. Thousands of new homes were erected with funds from government and cooperative credit associations. The farms had from eight to twenty acres, new spacious and comfortable buildings, machinery and good cattle. To become owners of such farms required a capital of only $250.00. There is no payment on principal for five years. In 1924 when the present Stauning Cabinet came into power with the Socialist-Democrats, further reductions of large estates took place so that today there are

20,000 more small farm owners than there were in
1915. This accounts for much of Denmark's prosperity.
A family of five can make a comfortable living on ten
acres of well-tilled land. Large families are becoming
rare in Denmark.

This great political influence has gone out from the
many small communities where men and women are
taught a sense of justice that benefits the city man as
well as the farmer. In a country like Denmark where
agriculture is the main occupation, prosperity of the
farmer means prosperity for the city. This holds true
of North Dakota also, and, in fact, of every agricultural
state. Denmark, then, has benefited by the intelligent
and conservative influence of the People's College. Half
of the present twelve members of the Danish Cabinet
are former students of the People's College.

Community Education.—Hand in hand with political
influence, Grundtvig wanted community educational influence. He had addressed people in rural schools, at
open-air meetings, and in meeting houses. He had ad-
vocated a new type of community center where education could continue. To him education was a lifelong
process and provisions should therefore be made available for its continuation. To do this Grundtvig realized
that there was a danger of radicalism and destructive
influences. To avoid any unfortunate beginning, he
recommended to the students of the People's College,
which then were very conservative, that they, after
having been enlightened and enlivened, go out to their
respective communities and gather the people to form
an Educational Community Association. Through local
subscriptions funds were collected for the erection of a
meeting house (Forsamlingshus) in which all had a
share and an interest. Within a few years no less than
1,000 organizations had constructed large halls in which

to hold their educational meetings. Soon they were recognized as community centers.

Naturally, the students who had been intellectually awakened through the informal and inspirational lectures by the teachers at the People's Colleges thought first of how they themselves could continue to have the opportunity to listen to such men and women and also how others who had not been as privileged as they, might benefit by hearing the cultured men of Scandinavia, Germany, England, and America. These students, therefore, became the leaders in the Lecture Societies of which there were, in 1937, one thousand one hundred.

The program launched by these **Lecture Societies** was at first purely educational. Men of note and of various occupations lectured on educational, social, political, historical, scientific, and agricultural topics. Not infrequently lectures were given on cooperatives. Often the meetings would be followed by a discussion under a capable leader, generally a former People's College student. At least ten meetings were held during the year. As would be expected, some of the lectures were, and are, not what might be desired. Many of the societies have become more social than educational in purpose. Still the people continue to give their moral and financial support to this worthy community enterprise. The attendance often reaches eighty-five per cent of the adult population, which shows that young and old unite in the lifelong process of learning. These societies have also aided in cooperation and understanding within the community. At the lecture meetings the people sit together, listen together and discuss together. Together they are interested in the improvement of themselves, their community, and their country. In unity they realize their strength.

Closely connected with lecture societies is the **library movement.** The students do little reading while at the People's College but Grundtvig was right in his contention that if youth were awakened and consequently became interested in knowledge, he would seek for himself the wisdom needed from day to day. Through the efforts of former students, libraries found their way into practically every community. As an example these students had their own private library. The Danish people now constitute a nation of readers. Someone has figured that the average Dane reads ten books, magazines and newspapers to the American's one. Although the writer doubts the full validity of this statement, the fact remains that the rural population reads much. There are sixty farm papers, many of which are dailies. Often we find farmers with two and even three daily newspapers with various political affiliation. This gives him a broad point of view.

At the community library, which is generally located in a special room in the Forsamlingshus or at the public school, he can get the books that are too expensive for the average private library. It cannot be said of any rural district that it has no library service. To compare this favorable condition with that of the United States, it has been found that:

> According to figures given by the American Library Association there are 5,954 public libraries in the 3,065 counties in the United States. But 1,135 counties have no public libraries within their borders. It is estimated that 45,069,897 people are without public library service. Of these 42,152,291, or 93 per cent are rural (living in the open country or in places having less than 2,500 population). Eighty-two per cent of the rural population of the United States do not have public library service, as compared with six per cent of the urban population who do not have such service.[1]

---

[1] The United States Department of Agriculture, "Farmer's Bulletin," No. 1559, 1928, p. 4.

These figures speak of the need of a rural library movement similar to that inaugurated by the students from the People's College in the decade following 1870. Grundtvig read and wrote much, his followers heeded his admonition that "reading, thinking, and writing makes a man wise and perfect."

In the public library in the Danish community, special attention is given to books on music. Many libraries contain large collections of **choral compositions,** sufficient in number to supply the local choral union. Since the Viking period, the Danish people have been a nation of singers. The early Sagas and the outstanding characters in Norse mythology were revived by Grundtvig in many of his 1000 poems. Grundtvig taught the rural people to sing songs in groups and while alone. An early riser traveling in the country might hear a song like this coming from the man walking behind the plough:

> The sun is rising in the east,
> It fills the heavens wide,
> And scatters light on mountain-crest,
> On shore and country-side.

Or in the hours of eventide the farmer with his family on the lawn might sing:

> The country lies in deep repose,
> And peace rules hearth and home,
> While silver clouds the moon inclose
> And through the heavens roam.

Thus Grundtvig and his good friend Ingemann gave to the rural population the inspiring songs that have lightened the burden of the daily tasks and brought new courage and strength. The farmer sings also with a group. Each community has its choir or glee club, which in numerous instances is directed by a former student of or teacher at the People's College. Singing, which plays an important part in the life of the college, generally becomes a part of the student the remaining years of his life. This influence the student brings into the community to be transferred to others in form of actual music instruction and appreciation.

Closely connected with music are **folkdancing and gymnastic societies.** Often the same individuals take part in all three. The folkdances (Folkedanse) are a type of figure and formation dance where several couples dance together. Practices are held twice a month. On the evening of the yearly performance national costumes are frequently used.

Gymnastics were formerly taught for military drill but about the year 1880 the People's Colleges adopted the Swedish system developed by Pehr Henrik Ling. This system changed the spirit of gymnastics. The aim became one of self-improvement and self-control. The system stresses orderly and controlled bodily motions; it develops strength and endurance and in the words of Trier, director of "Vallekilde Højskole", it teaches youth to "subordinate his body to his will."

The Swedish system has in recent years been developed further by Niels Bukh, director of Ollerup Gymnastic and Swimming College. With his team he has visited America, Australia, Japan, and other countries. Many, fearing a return to the Spartan idea of the body, have criticized this institution. It cannot be denied, however, that Niels Bukh has been instrumental in raising the level of wholesome physical exercises.

The **target-practice union** (Skytteforening), like gymnastics, is a non-military organization. The purpose of this practice is for the sake of sport and enjoyment, and to develop marksmanship. An annual competition takes place between the district organizations. Special prizes are given to the best marksmen.

All of the activities mentioned so far are a part of community education. All of them are direct or indirect contributions by the People's College toward the building of a real community. They have all had their share in raising the cultural standard of the people. But there is one more enterprise in community education which must not be overlooked, namely that of the **Evening School Union.** In 1936 approximately 25,000 adolescents and youths attended these evening sessions. During the two-hour session held twice a week, courses in Danish language and literature, foreign languages, drawing, surveying, arithmetic, and other practical subjects are offered. The tuition is $2.50 for the year with special government aid to pay instructors and supplies. As a rule the courses are presented in the public school.

Although only a small number of students from People's Colleges teach in these evening sessions, they have, nevertheless, given them their moral support. The persons who attend the evening courses find work at the People's Colleges more understandable and profitable. This work serves as a fine introduction to cultural courses.

In the foregoing paragraphs the making of an educational community has been traced to the cultural influence of the People's Colleges. Ever since the year 1866 this influence has continued by supplying men and women with firm hopes and convictions in the betterment of the individual and social and economic conditions. These men and women have dared tackle the grave problems of human life as a corporate body, realizing that in unity of purpose there is great strength. They have applied themselves and their life energy to rise above ignorance, poverty, and provincialism, and, as we shall observe in the next chapter, they have been willing to make adjustments that required sacrifices in order to improve the condition of the group as a whole. This they have done of their own accord and without regimentation from the government or private authorities.

Mr. Hart, in speaking of the community and the People's College, says:

> And so—we come back to the folk high-schools with their seventy-five years of actual history in the village and the country-side; with their unquestionable achievements in releasing and developing the understanding of the individual and the community; with their sturdy promise that, even for the future, they will release and discipline the native intelligence needed for the control of the emerging new conditions in life and economy and industrial relationships. The folk school and the folk community are inseparable; they are—in a very real sense—not two entities but a single reality looked at izing the whole content of country life. [2]

Mrs. Campbell, Director of the John C. Campbell Folk School at Brasstown, North Carolina, writes:

> These short-term schools for young adults have succeeded to a remarkable degree in arousing and enlightening the rural population, and in dignifying and vitalizing the whole content of country life.[1]

In referring to the high intelligence of the Danish rural population, the Norwegian poet, Bjornson, uses these superlative words: "The most intelligent peasantry in the world." [3]

---

[1] Hart, "Light From The North," p. 104.
[2] Campbell, "The Danish Folk School," p. viii.
[3] Hegland, "The Danish People's High School, p. 130.

CHAPTER V

CONTRIBUTION OF THE PEOPLE'S COLLEGE

II. SCIENTIFIC FARMING

A New Farm Spirit.—In the previous chapter we saw how the People's Colleges have influenced community education; but this is not the only influence attributed to these cultural institutions. It is generally admitted that these schools began the scientific farming that has become a model to the world. It requires no small amount of intelligence and knowledge of economics to rise from crude to scientific methods of farming in the course of fifty years.

The men active in the movement for an enlightened farm population realized after the disastrous war of 1864-1866, in which Denmark lost a large strip of land,[1] that crop raising and stock breeding had to be improved in order to redeem the loss. The **Danish Heath Society** was formed in 1866 to reclaim the waste lands of Northern and Central Jutland. Under the able leadership of Enrico Mylius Dalgas about 3000 square miles, an area larger than that lost to Germany, has been converted into good farm land.

To improve farming conditions in general, **Agricultural Societies** were formed under the unselfish leader-

---

[1] In 1864-66 Denmark lost North Slesvig to Germany, an area of about 3000 square miles. The land reclaimed from heath was more than 3000 square miles.

ship of People's College directors and students. These societies (Landboforeninger and Husmandsforeninger) had one common interest—the educational and scientific improvement of agriculture. In 1937 no less than 91 per cent of the 207,000 Danish farmers belonged to these societies. This tremendous progress can only be accounted for by the fact that the leaders were trusted men worthy of full support. The Danish farmers soon learned the advantage of working together for a common good. To them the improvement of agriculture became this common good. The individual farmer became willing to make adjustments for the good of the society as a whole.

New Methods.—The first adjustment to be made in the two decades following 1870, was the **change from grain to dairying.** Cheap grain was being imported by Denmark and other countries, from the prairies of America and the lowlands of Russia. Realizing that they could not compete with these great nations, the Danish farmers turned to cattle raising. Purebred stock was imported from England and Belgium. By 1890 the change was complete and Denmark was exporting huge quantities of bacon, eggs, butter and cheese to England, Germany, America, and other countries. In 1937 eighty-five per cent of the herds consisted of purebred stock. The goal is to have 100 per cent by 1950. Special assistance is given by the government to replace tubercular cattle with pure stock. In 1936, the livestock consisted of 520,000 horses, 3,000,000 cattle, 3,000,000 swine, and 30,000,000 chickens.[1]

In order to raise the most profitable stock, **Cow Testing Associations** (organized 1895) were formed

---

[1] "World Almanac," 1938, p. 618.

throughout the country. These associations employ an agricultural and dairy expert who has been educated at a People's College or Agricultural College to have charge of about 1,000 cows. Once each three weeks or once a month, depending upon the amount of farms in the associations, the expert comes to the farm, weighs and tests the milk from each cow. He also weighs the amount of feed given each cow in order to determine at the end of the year the cost of feeding and the income. Often this expert advises the farmer to sell a cow which did not show sufficient profit to warrant its keeping. The farmer who is interested in the bidgest possible yield at the least expense generally heeds the advice. Thus today the visitor at a Danish barn will find a tablet above the stall of each cow with a record of when the cow was born, number of calves born, amount of feed consumed, quantity and quality of milk produced.

The expert also gives advice on the general condition and upkeep of the farm, such as quality of grain, types of fertilizers, and bull to be used for breeding. That the farmer benefits from such expert advice there is little doubt. For all this service on the economic status of his farm the owner pays not more than fifty cents (two kroner) per year for each cow.

In the matter of grain raising the Danish farmer has improved both in tilling the soil, in the use of manure, and Chile and Norway saltpeter **(commercial fertilizers)**. Even a small farm of six acres has a **rotation of crops.** The rotation is generally as follows: First year, wheat; second year, barley; third year, root crops; fourth year, oats; fifth and sixth year, grass; seventh year no crop but plowed several times to kill weeds and mix soil with fertilizer. The eighth year the farmer sows wheat again. This rotation has proved to bring a greater yearly yield.

Of the area of Denmark in 1935, 31 per cent was in wheat, rye, barley, and oats; 11.86 per cent in sugar beets and root crops for feed; 17.15 per cent in forest; and the remaining 19.89 per cent consisted of heath, chalk, and marsh lands, besides the area occupied by cities.[1]

The yield of grain and potatoes in bushels for 1936 was as follows:

Wheat	14,672,000
Rye	11,177,000
Barley	50,478,000
Oats	71,787,000
Potatoes	45,282,000

The sugar beet yield in 1935 was 233,162 metric tons.[2]

Comparing the yield of wheat per acre with that of America it is found that Denmark raises an average of 44.4 bushels to the acre and America 13.7.[3] This difference is undoubtedly due partly to weather and soil conditions. But the Danish farmer realizes that where he takes so much out of the ground he must put something in. His success is also due to his great care in preparing the soil and in his method of crop rotation.

Important Factors.—An important factor in the success of the Danish farmer, who is enjoying general prosperity even after the world economic depression of 1929, is that of **land ownership.** As early as 1850 a credit association was organized on a cooperative basis, in order to aid renters in becoming owners. Land ownership was looked upon as being fundamental to agri-

---

[1] "Hvem, Hvad, Hvor," Politikken, 1937, p. 102.
[2] "World Almanac," 1938, p. 618.
[3] "Yearbook of Agriculture," 1935, p. 356.

cultural progress. It was found that the owner took much more interest and pride in his farm than the renter. Renting was a hindrance to the introduction of new scientific methods of farming. This hindrance, however, was gradually overcome by purchasing farms for private ownership. In 1850 only 45 per cent of the farmers owned the land they worked as compared with 90 per cent in 1937. In other words, of the 207,000 farmers in Denmark in 1937, 186,300 owned their land.

Private land ownership in America has been decreasing especially since the economic disaster of 1929 when the low prices on farm products failed to meet the high interest and payment on loans. The American farmer had no credit association with collective liability to give him security as did the Danish farmer. The result has been a reduction in private ownership and an increase in tenancy.

The following figures compiled by the United States Census of Agriculture, 1935, show the percentage of farms operated by tenants in a few representative states:

	1930	1935
Kansas	42.4	44.0
Illinois	43.1	44.5
South Dakota	44.6	48.6
Nebraska	47.1	49.3
Iowa	47.3	49.6
Georgia	68.2	65.9
Mississippi	72.2	69.8

In 1937 only about fifty per cent of the farmers owned their land as compared with Denmark's ninety per cent.

Another factor to be reckoned with in the success of the Danish farmer in developing scientific methods is that of **living at one place for a long period** of years and the **economic security** thus obtained, as compared with the mobile farm population in America. The value of the farm land in America in 1935 amounted to $32,-858,844,012, while the total farm mortgage indebtedness was $7,645,891,000.[1] The latter figure, however, does not include loans which corporations held on their own farms. The federal government has taken steps to help the tenant farmer to own his land. In 1937 loans of $10,000,000 were available and in 1939 this sum will be increased to $25,000,000 for farm purchases. This sum will remain at $50,000,000 annually following 1939.[2]

Such steps will undoubtedly lessen the mobile farm population and aid in creating economic security. In the **Yearbook of Agriculture** for 1935 we read: "From the standpoint of better land use and also of better rural welfare, we need to correct the unwholesome features of tenancy. These are the migratory habits it fosters, and the disregard of soil fertility and long-time farm efficiency. In this country the average occupancy of farm tenants is about two or three years as compared with average owner occupancy of about fourteen years.[3] It is quite self-evident from this situation that there are great obstacles to the development of scientific farming. The writer is of the opinion that the problem of tenancy can be overcome in part by the creation of common liability credit associations under which loans would be given to farmers at a low interest and over a long period of years.

Regarding the progress which the Danish farmer has made the last sixty years, Mr. Hart says:

> Something has happened in the Danish countryside that has not happened elsewhere in the world; the farmer has become the **scientist in his work** and the cooperator in his economic life, and through science and co-

---

[1] "World Almanac," 1938, p. 346.

[2] "Ibid.," p. 347.

[3] "Yearbook of Agriculture," 1935, p. 67.

operation he has achieved—within the limits and stabilities of the existent world order—such a control over his own destiny as to be rightly called "independent." These results are, quite naturally, by the Danes and their visitors, predominantly, attributed to the work of these independent, free schools, which have violated all the accepted practices of the conventional schools and universities; but which have helped thereby to secure to the private and public life of Denmark an intellectual depth and breadth almost unknown elsewhere—not primarily by working for it in a formal fashion, but by making such a result supremely desirable as a community accomplishment and by eliminating those obstacles which in most schools stand in the way of progress to the goals they most profess to be seeking.[1]

---

[1] Hart, "Light From The North," pp. 38, 39.

CHAPTER VI

CONTRIBUTION OF THE PEOPLE'S COLLEGE

III. COOPERATIVES

At the beginning of this chapter on cooperation a few statements regarding the origin of cooperatives seem appropriate. It was Robert Owen, the impractical idealist, who between 1820 and 1840 tried to organize cooperative societies in England. By 1840 not one of his societies functioned. But in 1843 the weavers of Rochdale, living on forty-five cents a week, planned very carefully a consumers' cooperative which became a great success. This humble beginning expanded to all parts of England and its influence has been felt in most parts of the world.

What were the basic principles of the Rochdale Cooperative which proved successful? The following fundamental principles served as foundation for the Danish cooperatives:

Universality
Open membership. Only restrictions those dictated by self-preservation and safety.
No sex, race, color or creed lines to be recognized as far as membership in the cooperative is concerned.
Movement to be not only national but also international in scope, with the final aim of comprising the whole world.
Education in the universality of the movement.

Democracy
Each member, both man and woman, to have only one vote in the affairs of the cooperative.

No proxy voting to be permitted.

Frequent membership and board meetings. Regular reports from executives and administrative committees.

Constant educational work to stir up interest among members in the affairs of their organization; to educate members for democratic control; to bring in new members and patrons; to increase efficiency of administration.

Fair treatment of labor. Encouragement of employees to become active members of the cooperative employing them.

Provisions in the by-laws of the cooperative safe-guarding democratic control.

Access to membership in the cooperative to be made easy (through shares of low par value, etc.).

Equity

Capital to be given no special privileges. When employed it should be given a "fair wage" in the form of a fixed, current legal interest. If capital can be attracted without any interest reward, so much the better.

Net earnings to be distributed not to stockholders on the basis of their capital investment but to patrons in proportion to their patronage. Patronage refunds to non-member patrons to be applied toward a share until a full share is acquired.

Goods handled to be pure, unadulterated and of good quality.

Full weight and measure to be given at all times.

Equal and fair treatment of all patrons. No favoritism.

No credit to be given, nor asked for. Cash trade, as the fairest method, to be practiced zealously.

Economy

Cash trade to be favored as it is also the most economical method. Constant educational work to be carried on in favor of cash trade.

Efficient management. Minimum waste and duplication. Constant training of cooperative employees to increase their efficiency.

Accurate bookkeeping.

Periodical auditing by competent cooperatively-minded auditors, with the view of improving efficiency and getting better business results.

Ample depreciations and reserves.

No business competition between the cooperatives to be tolerated.

Publicity

Honesty in all affairs of the cooperative. No business secrets.

Frequent and comprehensive reports.

Dissemination of information among the members about the affairs and the true condition of the cooperative. Encouragement of constructive criticism to eliminate defects and weaknesses.

Continuous efforts to spread the cooperative message among the consumers.

Unity

Tolerance among the members of the cooperative toward each other's views on politics, religion, etc.

Constant endeavor on part of members to be kind and fair toward each other; to be calm, considerate and level-headed at the meetings of the cooperative; to avoid stirring up trouble and questioning the motives of the other fellow.

Keeping controversial issues of a political or religious nature out of the meetings of the cooperative. Policy of strict neutrality toward political parties, churches, by the cooperative society as an organization.

Doing away, through education, with racial and nationalistic prejudices. Recognition of the principle of brotherhood of man, irrespective of race or color.

Encouragement of cooperation between the cooperatives.

Development of regional, district and national unions and international federations of the cooperatives.

Liberty

Membership to be voluntary. Withdrawal to be made easy.

Democratic administration and control in place of autocratic or bureaucratic control.

Persuasion in place of coercion. No "iron-clad" contracts to bind the members.

Intensive education in cooperation to create interest, loyalty, and devotion in place of ignorance and indifference.

Economic liberty and security through intelligent cooperation. Recognition of the fact that economic security is the best guarantee of individual liberty.[1]

Although these principles concern the consumers' cooperatives specifically they have formed the basis for cooperatives in general. Furthermore, the Rochdale principles served as the basis for the first cooperative organization in Denmark.

---

[1] Alanne, Summary of the Rochdale Principles, "Fundamentals of Consumer Cooperation, pp. 44-45.

The Spirit of Cooperation in Denmark.—The most outstanding contribution of the People's College to Denmark and to the world at large is the highly developed system of cooperation, a system of real cooperation which in some instances includes ninety per cent of the people. Although the cooperative movement was started in England about the year 1830 and brought to Denmark twenty years later by a clergyman, Dean Sonne, who was interested in the development of credit associations, it has reached a higher degree of perfection in Denmark than perhaps anywhere else in the world. Kagawa the Japanese Christian-social reformer, says of Denmark that it "is the most Christian country in the world because of the excellent balance it has between the consumer and producer sides of the cooperative movements. The Danish farmer is a member of five or six different sorts of cooperatives at the same time. Practically all his economic operations are carried on cooperatively, and his income, from being one of the worst, has, in about eighty years, risen to be the best average income of all the farmers in Europe."[1] This remarkable advancement must be attributed to the work of the People's College, as we shall see in this chapter.

Webster's Dictionary defines cooperation as "the act of cooperating, or of operating together to one need; joint operation; concurrent effort of labor." This definition might well apply to the People's Colleges. Cooperation is the very core of all of their activities. Without it, their work would fail. Although several of the institutions have left the conservative path outlined by Grundtvig, especially that of religion, yet they have maintained that cooperative spirit which is so essential to progress in a democratic nation. Many of the students at these schools, it must be admitted, do not receive any

---

[1] From a leaflet, 1937.

good from the cultural education presented. This is partly due to the lack of a cooperative conception of life. When the Great Teacher said, "No man liveth unto himself," he spoke a truth fundamental for human progress.

Influence of the People's Colleges on Cooperatives.— When Grundtvig began his work in education, he found a nation of disheartened and aimless people scattered by internal and external conflicts. Denmark had lost its power and prestige. There was no person "for such a time as this" (Esther 4:14) and no institution to unify the nation broken in spirit. The state had proved itself unable to meet the situation; education was for the few born into the upper classes; the church was filled with dead orthodox theology and rationalism; and the farmers were largely tenants and laborers hired by large land owners. But as practically every national crisis in human history has produced some individual to meet the situation, so also Denmark had its national hero in the troublesome eighteenth century. Fortunate for the Danish people the task fell to a man who loved the people and who had their welfare at heart more than personal gain, honor, and power. Although Grundtvig did belong to the aristocracy he renounced his social position to identify himself with the common people, and thereby gradually raise them to a higher level of intelligence. To accomplish this feat he at once realized the need of the cooperation of the parties concerned. About 1840 the people of Denmark wanted better government and more justice. But the farmers in Jutland did not agree with the farmers on Funen and Zealand on how this was to be accomplished. The same disagreement existed within other groups to the detriment of all. It was this discouraging situation which caused Grundtvig to give a series of lectures throughout the nation on the history of Denmark, the need of an intellectual enlightenment of the common people, and the necessity of cooperating for a common good. These lectures stirred the people to action. In 1844 the first People's College was founded at Rødding, Southern Jutland. Five years later the Danish people were given a constitution. Before 1860 the first Cooperative Credit Association was organized. By 1875 almost 100 People's Colleges had been founded; and by 1885 consumer and producer cooperatives had found an important place in the business life of country and city. This remarkable story of progress reads almost as the story of mechanical progress in the United States.

The riches of Denmark were few, but as Kold often said, "Where there is little there is room for God's blessing." Grundtvig wished to preserve the "little," to multiply it, and to better it. To do this the people had to realize the value of the "little" and to know how to increase and improve it. This necessitated general enlightenment of the farmer and the worker so that they might fill their place in the great development of human and natural resources. The People's College became the means to this end.

The People's Colleges have no special course on cooperatives as they are an integral part of all subjects that lend themselves to such an interpretation and application. The writers of textbooks, teachers, and students are **cooperative conscious.** Although human history is primarily the record of great characters, and the Danish history teacher enjoys to stress the importance of great men and women, yet the success of these characters must be attributed to the cooperation of many common people or their failure due to lack of cooperation. In both cases, reasons for or lack of cooperation are carefully studied. Such study forms an excellent basis for a discussion of local and national cooperatives and reasons for their success or failure. Discussions by enlightened future leaders often result in suggestions for improvement of cooperatives. Lectures on agriculture have largely the same result, only in such courses more direct applications are made to the cooperatives. The actual operation is considered carefully for the purpose of pointing out national, local, and individual benefits. Often special lectures are given to draw the attention of the students to the implications of cooperatives—for example, their effect upon people's morale, international trade, property ownership, rural and city life, agricultural efficiency, financial benefits and other important effects.

Besides the above mentioned direct teaching of cooperation the spirit of the institution is of a cooperative character. Since attendance at these schools is voluntary, calling for no examinations at the beginning, during, or at the end of the school term, and promising no diploma, cooperation is expected on the part of teachers and students alike in and out of the classroom. Therefore, indirect teaching of cooperation by example is an important factor in the life of these schools and their success depends upon it. Often teachers and students will be in a snowball contest and ten minutes later all will gather in the lecture hall to sing together the songs that unite in one common goal—the enrichment of life. An hour later all may share a simple meal in the college dining room. That such shared activities inculcate the meaning and value of cooperation in the student is quite natural. It becomes a part of him and later finds expression in his daily life and activities on the farm and in the community. In this connection H. Hertel, a writer of the history of Danish cooperation, who has no personal contact with the People's Colleges

of Denmark, has summed up the influence of Grundtvig's and Kold's schools in the following words:

> These schools awakened in young men and women a
> yearning for knowledge and a desire to work; the charac-
> ter of the pupils was strengthened, and they left the
> schools with a much enlarged outlook on life. To satisfy
> its yearning for knowledge, a current of youth flowed
> from the folk high schools to the agriculture schools,
> and when it afterwards passed out into life it did so
> with a strong feeling of fellowship, and a desire to work
> for common progress. Youth thus gained some of the
> qualifications necessary to the success of a cooperative
> movement.[1]

The term cooperatives is wide in meaning and quite
inclusive as will be noticed from its present usage. In
this chapter the main interest is centered on the question: What **kind** of cooperatives have these enlivened
and enlightened students from the People's Colleges
produced? In this connection a few examples will be
cited of how the cooperatives operate.

The Organization of Cooperatives.—The most distinct
feature which characterizes all the Danish cooperatives
is the **common** or **collective liability.** This formed an
integral part of the first credit cooperatives. The members would together share the benefit or the loss of the
association. Great care was shown in the matter of
investment and the credit association (Kreditforening)
experienced few losses. When the world-wide economic
depression came in 1929 the association was sufficiently
powerful to take any possible loss. This common responsibility has had a wholesome psychological effect
upon the farmers. They assume responsibilities and
maintain them through critical periods. They have
learned that in unity and cooperation there is great
strength.

A second characteristic of the Danish cooperatives is
their **democratic spirit.** The smallest unit has its repre-

[1] Hertel, "Andelsbevægelsen i Danmark, p. 565.

sentation on the district board, and the district has its representation on the national board. The power of the cooperatives is vested in the local unit rather than in the national organization. The interest of the individual is the interest of the national group. Now and then individuals and even districts will make adjustments for the good of all groups. What is for the best of the group as a whole is also best for all in the course of time. This mutual and democratic spirit permeates the Danish organizations.

A third characteristic is the **quality of products** produced. The members of the cooperatives soon realized that if they were to compete with the established egg companies, for example, they would have to produce a better and guaranteed quality. The members bought the best hens to be had, gave them good feed, sent the eggs regularly to collecting plants, and did everything to produce first-class eggs. In order to guarantee the eggs to be fresh, the cooperatives began to mark the eggs. First the number of the farm (and sometimes the farmer stamps the number of the hen that laid the egg), then a small letter of the alphabet to designate the local collector, which is followed by a large letter of the alphabet to designate the district. If a housewife in London should happen to buy a spoiled egg in one of the cooperative stores, the egg, through its numbering, could be traced back to the farmer who sold it and even to the hen which laid the egg.

A fourth characteristic is that the Danish cooperatives, although unincorporated, are built on a **sound economic plan** in which every member is morally and financially responsible. No cooperative union, except one, which later failed, has as yet been organized before assurance had been given of sufficient members and volume of business. Any loans made for operating expenses are guaranteed by the members in the union. This responsibility, however, seldom goes beyond the local community. Whenever a national loan is desired, a limit of liability is generally set by the local cooperative. In case of a dispute the difficulty is settled by a board of arbitration which consists of members of the involved associations.

A fifth characteristic of the Danish cooperative movement is its **beginning in individual communities** rather than as a national organization. There is one exception to this procedure—namely that of the Danish Cooperative Potato Association. This association established in 1919 began with a central office and then organized local collecting stations, but it failed two years later. The local cooperative unit is the basis for the progress of the national cooperative. The members pledge themselves to send all products to the local plant. This is also true of the consumer's cooperative. The usual duration of such voluntary pledges is generally from one to twenty years. Seldom does anyone withdraw his pledge with the local cooperative.

The strength of the local units can be traced to the influence of students from the People's Colleges. These students are interested in the welfare of the people who produce and consume the goods. Their sense of justice is such that only fairness to all parties concerned will be permitted. These farmer students are generally the leaders, because they have the ability to express themselves and the organizing ability that makes for success. Therefore, what the Danish cooperatives are in spirit and organization is ultimately due to the work of the People's Colleges.

The most prominent cooperative associations organized in Denmark are: Bacon, Breeding, Cow-testing, Credit, Dairy, Egg, Fertilizer, Grocery, Rural and National Banks, and the Seed Growers' Cooperative Association.

How do these cooperatives in Denmark operate? This question is often asked by the foreigner interested in cooperatives. Individuals and groups have come from all parts of the world to observe the Danish cooperatives in action. Since space does not permit a consideration of all the cooperatives, we shall, therefore, as example refer to one producers' cooperative and one consumers' cooperative.

The Dairy Cooperatives (Andelsmejerier) of Denmark can be traced to a mere incident. About 1850 the large land owners had begun to export butter to England, but no consideration was given to the small farmer. The quantities he produced were too small for recognition on the English market. This realization led some of them to establish collecting stations where each farmer could bring his butter. Although this was a step forward, it was soon found that the quality was not the same from each farm. This was a disadvantage as compared with the large farmer who, from a herd of 200 cows, could ship the same quality even though his butter was not superior. Little recognition was given the small farmer on the English market until a former People's College student, a small farmer in West Jutland, with a herd of six cows, sent a sample of butter to the International Agricultural Exhibition in London in 1879. At this exhibition this small farmer won first prize. The recognition served as an excellent impetus to the small farmers of Denmark. Three years later the first Cooperative Creamery was organized at Hjedding, West Jutland.

The method of organizing the Hjedding Cooperative is the one followed today. A survey is made of the township (Sogn) to determine the possibility of establishing a creamery. If it is found that there are from 800 to 900 cows in the township, each farmer is invited to a meeting where each has one vote in deciding for or against a cooperative creamery. Membership is voluntary. If there is sufficient interest in the organization, a constitution is formed in which each farmer pledges himself to support the creamery financially and with delivery of milk. A central location for the creamery is chosen, milk routes are outlined, and a dairy expert employed to manage the creamery. Generally, a farmer, living at the beginning of the milk route, will collect the sweet milk in the morning and return skim milk or buttermilk by noon. For this service he is paid from $300 to $600 per year. The usual number of milk routes to one creamery is fourteen. Of all the milk delivered, ninety-five per cent is used for butter-making.

The cooperative creamery holds annual meetings in which elections are held. Each farmer, whether he delivers a thousand pounds of milk or a hundred thousand pounds, has but one vote. The members are not stockholders and have no shares in the creamery. Their financial support means merely security for the loan made for initial building and operating expenses. This loan is reduced by the yearly surplus. The farmers pool expenses and surpluses annually. Often a farmer with a herd of eighteen purebred cows will have an annual benefit or dividend amounting to $400. This he receives besides getting the regular price for his milk. The annual income from the 1400 cooperative dairies amounts to about $30,000,000. In this huge income ninety per cent of the Danish farmers have a share.

As a rule the farmer pledges himself to deliver milk to the cooperative creamery from ten to twenty years. The milk must be clean and of good quality. The Danish cow barns are cleaned every day, washed once a week, and white-washed at least once a year. The milk must not be kept on the farm more than twenty-four hours. The milk cans are thoroughly washed and scalded once a day. If the milk is sour or dirty when it reaches the creamery, it is returned to the farmer. The manager, having at least one assistant and an apprentice, tests the milk at least once a week and observes it closely each day before pouring it into the collecting basin. All these precautions and requirements are made for the purpose of producing the best quality of butter and cheese. In this attempt the Danish cooperative creameries have succeeded. The first prize won at the London exhibition in 1879 was the forerunner of a long list of first prizes to be awarded the Danish farmer for his efforts to better food products, and thereby protect the consumer's health.

Although the average cooperative creamery has a membership of 150 farmers, and receives about 4,500,000 pounds of milk annually, some of the plants have grown immensely. For example, Trifolium Creamery in Haslev, the largest in Denmark and one of the largest in the world, has a staff of fifty creamery experts, receives an average of 60,000 pounds of milk per day, has space for 50,000 cheeses, and sends cheese to all parts of the globe, including the United States. Trifolium has in recent years, together with a few other creameries, entered the business of producing condensed milk and powdered milk. A special plant has been erected for this purpose.

The cooperative creameries of Denmark are organized into a **Federation of Cooperative Creameries.** This organization exists for export purposes and unification of prices. Better prices are paid for large shipments. The farmers had this experience already in 1875. The

Federation exists also for uniformity of quality. Even though the butter is packed in fir barrels in the local creameries, samples are voluntarily sent to the main office of the Federation at regular intervals. Comments on the quality are returned following each test and inspection. The price of the butter is determined by the quality and the grade to which it belongs. If it reaches the required standard it is marked with the words "Lur Brand" and "Danish Butter." "Lur" is an old Danish word for war trumpets. After passing a favorable inspection the butter was formerly sold by the Federation to an exchange which would then export the butter to foreign countries. But today the Federation of Producers' Cooperative Creameries of Denmark can sell the butter to a consumers' cooperative in England. This arrangement has completely eliminated any profit by the middleman. The profit is equally shared by the one who produced and the one who consumes the products.

The Danish Consumers' Cooperative Association has developed much since 1900. Its annual turnover of business is about $65,000,000 annually from the almost 1,900 consumers' cooperatives. It was organized by an economist in Copenhagen as early as 1850. This economist, Frederik Dreier (1827-1853), who had observed the cooperatives in England was asked by the workers to establish a cooperative store. This he did but the undertaking failed for lack of support from the workers. It was not until 1866 that the cooperative store was organized on a sound business basis by Rev. H. C. Sonne in the home town of Kristen Kold. Like other cooperatives it had its beginning in the rural districts.

The underlying principles of the consumers' cooperative store are the same as those of the producers' cooperatives. Membership is voluntary; each member has one vote; collective liability for all loans is assumed by all. Such loans are paid by the annual surplus. At the annual meeting the board is elected which in turn employs a manager. The members pledge themselves to support the store for at least ten years. All dividends are paid annually and are exempt from income taxes.

In order to show the extent of cooperatives in Denmark we shall list the various organizations, approximate number of organizations, and year formed:

Kind of Cooperative	Number of Organizations (approximately)	Year Organized
Food-stuff Societies	1,387	1851
Dairies	1,400	1882
Dairy Societies	800	1887
Milk Testing Associations	400	1902
Danish Dairy Butter-seal Societies	1,400	1900
Bacon Factories	62	1887
The United Bacon Factories	60	1890
Danish Egg Export	700	1895
Potato Export	15	1913
Butter Export	10	1888
Cattle Export	15	1898
Danish Bacon Company	1	1912
Cattle Breeding Associations	700	1881
Horse Breeding Associations	400	1879
Swine Breeding Associations	200	1882
Sheep Breeding Associations	150	1899
Goat Breeding Associations	60	1909
Cow-testing Associations	1,750	1892
Consumers' Societies	1,824	1872
Credit Associations	14	(1775) 1850
Banking Associations	160	1897
The Cooperative Bank, Copenhagen	1	1913
Savings Associations	500	1884
Cattle Insurance Associations	2,500	1810
Bull Associations	1,400	1884
Hail Insurance Associations	20	1864
Storm Insurance Associations	10	1896
Fire Insurance Associations	10	1856
Accident Insurance Associations	(200,000 members)	1898
Life Insurance Associations	10	1904
Use of Machinery	2,000	1914
Electrical Plants	400	1895
Coal Supply Associations	600	1913

Kind of Cooperative	Number of Organizations (approximately)	Year Organized
Fertilizer Associations	1,450	1866
Bakeries	40	1888
Fruit Societies	20	1903
Sanatorium Associations	1,200	1904
Cement Associations	850	1911
Renting Associations	1	1912

Due to the policy of "building from the ground up" and vesting the power in the local unit rather than in a central organization, the mortality of Danish cooperatives has been very low.

The Cooperative Potato Association began in 1913 from a central organization. In one year it had about 350 local associations with almost 25,000 members. Prices were high and the organization paid a high dividend but neglected to lay aside any capital and was discontinued the next year when a depression came.

One Danish Cooperative bank was closed.

Great care has generally been exercised before starting cooperatives.

The Danish cooperatives have contributed much to the welfare of the rural districts. The people have assumed the responsibility of the middleman; they buy and sell in large quantities, thereby obtaining collective and individual benefits. They have succeeded in establishing a favorable distribution of wealth and power, which has maintained general prosperity in the midst of a world economic depression, and they have paid their taxes and improved their property with dividends from producers' and consumers' cooperatives. This success is due largely to the enlivened and enlightened youth who have come from the Danish People's Colleges.

What qualities did these farmer students possess which helped to make the cooperatives a success? There are four qualities which the People's Colleges aim to develop in the students:

1. Leadership and the ability to express oneself in word and deed.

2. Conservative but progressive ideas.

3. Knowledge of cooperatives and the true meaning of cooperation.

4. Unselfish interests for the welfare of Denmark.

As a conclusion to this discussion of cooperatives, we quote Dr. Einar Jensen, Principal Agricultural Economist, United States Department of Agriculture:

> In the past, Danish farmers have had to act in unison if they expected to "hold their own" against other classes of society. This natural spirit has been broadened by the activity of the folk schools. Through the teaching of history and its illustrations of the need for concerted action, the idea that the individual is also a part of the larger group of the nation and of the whole society has been strengthened. An attitude is created which is willing to forego petty, temporary gains in order to obtain greater advantages for all in the future, even if there may be minor differences in the sharing of these advantages. To the degree that this teaching succeeds, a favorable attitude is also created toward cooperation in general. It manifests itself in the numerous economic problems which call for cooperation. In such indirect ways have the folk schools been instrumental in the furtherance of cooperation.
>
> The schools have had a powerful influence on the farming class. They have provided the students with the means of constructing a philosophy of life characterized by simplicity and activity. They have increased self-respect, confidence, and a sense of independence, and stimulated rural Denmark to activity and constructive work at a time when such stimulus was much needed.[1]

Sir Michael Sadler, Master of University College, Oxford, gives this estimate of the influence which the People's Colleges have had on cooperatives:

> And it is universally admitted that the agricultural population could not, but for the work of the People's High Schools, have shown adaptability so great, open-

---

[1] Jensen, "Danish Agriculture," pp. 103-104.

mindedness so intelligent. Grundtvig's policy had found the issue he predicted. Corporate life in an atmosphere of liberal education had given practical culture. The new leaders of the peasantry, the organizers of the new and effective cooperation, were for the most part high school men. "The cooperative dairies," wrote Mr. Alfred Poulsen of Ryslinge, who read a memorable lecture at the Oxford Summer Meeting in August, 1894, "rose like magic." Butter and bacon saved Danish agriculture. Behind the new and swift reorganization of one of the most conservative and individualistic of industries were brains, leadership and unselfish public spirit. The People's High Schools inspired their pupils with energy and idealised labour. "We clenched our fists as we listened to the lectures and yearned to go out and set to work." In the schools the young men learned to trust one another. In cooperative enterprise they translated that trust into terms of associated credit. The schools gave them a wide outlook, opening in the pupils' minds new windows through which they looked out on the world. With this effective culture, and with the faith which went with it, the young men and young women saved Danish farming. "The schools awakened in them a yearning for knowledge and a desire to work."[1]

---

[1]Begtrup. "The Folk High-Schools of Denmark," pp. 9-10

CHAPTER VII

HISTORY OF DANISH FOLK HIGH SCHOOLS IN AMERICA

No Record of Folk High Schools Available.—So far no historical account has ever been recorded of the Danish Folk High Schools in America. Since it is the express purpose of this thesis to show that the ideas of Grundtvig and Kold, the originators of the Folk High School movement, are applicable to American conditions, the writer deems it advisable to give a brief historical sketch of each Folk High School established in America.

Difficulties in Collecting Material.—In collecting the historical material, the writer has used many sources. These were personal interviews and correspondence, questionnaires, examination of school bulletins, often only a single copy of school bulletins was available. Biographies of the high school leaders were also studied. In some instances where the school existed for a short time and was conducted in a parsonage, the writer found little trace as to organization, administration, curriculum, student activities and general condition of the school. Other schools published no bulletins and the director is either dead or now living in Denmark. Despite these difficulties, an attempt has been made in this chapter to give a brief statement about each school, its activities and its contributions. In cases where much material was available and the institution of considerable prominence, more space has naturally been given.

ELKHORN FOLK HIGH SCHOOL
Elkhorn, Iowa

Early History:—The first attempt to transplant the ideas of Grundtvig and Kold to American soil was made as early as 1878. This folk school was started in a log house in Elkhorn, Iowa. The purpose of this institution was to give young men and women a cultural and religious education. The school was organized at the request of Folk School leaders in Denmark. In 1877, these Danish friends sent $20 to America for a school. This small gift directed the attention of the Danes in America to their responsibility in making an educational and cultural contribution. The Danish Church now became interested and decided that same year to build a school modelled after Askov Folkehøjskole.

At first there was some disagreement as to the location. Reverend H. J. Pedersen, a prominent leader in Folk School movement in America, suggested that a vote be taken with United States one dollar bills and that the community which sent the most bills would get the institution. Elkhorn, Iowa, won the institution and in 1878 a two story wooden structure, large enough to accommodate the teachers and twenty students, was erected. This building burned in 1887 and a new and larger building was built.

On November 1, 1878, Elkhorn Folk School began with Rev. C. L. Kirkeberg, a Norwegian, as director, two assistant teachers and sixteen students. The number of students soon doubled. Summer school for girls was also conducted and with much success. The school was supported by private gifts and by the income from students. The financial support was therefore the most serious problem. The school was not accredited, although the courses offered were much like those in the state high school with the exception of special lectures in Danish on subjects of general interest, and Bible hours. The life of the school resembled that of a large family—all working together, eating together, and studying together. The evening lectures were well attended by the farmers in the immediate vicinity.

The students came from practically every state in the Union and most of them were between the ages of 18 and 25. Many spent more money in transportation to the school than the cost of the whole school term. But they were young men and women with sincere desires to learn and to better themselves. The one year course helped them to realize life's value and to understand their work.

New Ownership and Progress.—From 1882 to 1897, Reverend Kristian Anker was director and owner. Under his able leadership the school grew in size and influence. However, a mistake was undoubtedly made when more academic and commercial subjects were added at the expense of cultural and agricultural subjects. After the year of 1900 the school waned in importance and was later united with the Dana College, Blair, Nebraska, an instiution accredited by the state of Nebraska.

Influence.—Elkhorn Folk High School succeeded in influencing many students who later made contributions to American life. The whole community was influenced by the life and activities of the school. Weekly evening meetings were conducted by the teachers and students and often outside speakers were used for the local population. These meetings consisted of lectures, open forums with discussion, concerts, debates, plays, and various social activities. To the entire community the school was the intellectual, cultural, and social center.

ASHLAND HIGH SCHOOL
Ashland, Michigan

History.—In the woods of Michigan lies the little town of Ashland. This community was settled early by a number of Danes and developed into a regular colony. It was here that Reverend H. J. Pedersen in 1882, built Ashland High School. The building was constructed so that the ground floor served as apartment for the director and his family, the first story for classrooms and chapel, and the top floor for student quarters. A small home was added for the assistant teacher.

The director, Reverend H. J. Pedersen, had been a student at Kold's school in Ryslinge, Denmark, and was anxious to establish a similar institution in the United States. He secured a good assistant and opened the first winter term with success.

Serious Problems.—No sooner had he started the term than he was faced with two problems, the financial and that of getting students. The director owned the school, but depended on friends to give their support. Although many did send money, the contributions were not sufficient to maintain the school. Therefore, in 1888 the director wished to give the school to his assistant. But this the law forbade. He then sold it for 99 cents.

The problem of getting students was fully as serious as the financial. The director had depended upon young Danes from the manufacturing city of Grand Rapids to spend the idle winter months at Ashland High School. But the young men did not wish to leave the conveniences and amusement of the city during the winter. The attendance, therefore, was small, only about 20. The school was continued until 1902 when it became the parsonage of the local pastor.

Influence.—The school was the cultural center of the colony. Many students learned English and through the lectures were taught to live better lives and do better work.

WEST DENMARK HIGH SCHOOL
West Denmark, Wisconsin

The third Danish folk high school to be built in America was the one of West Denmark, Wisconsin, built in 1884. The Danish colony comprised West Denmark, Luck, Milltown, and Bone Lake. The school had a favorable location in the colony in the midst of great natural beauty. Reverend K. S. Norgaard became its first and only director as the school was closed in 1887.

The school was located so as to serve the local congregation; but its connection with the rest of the state was not favorable. Transportation was hardly possible to the school. It was soon found that the colony was not large enough to support a high school of its own. After three years of activity it was turned into a theological seminary and later became the parsonage of the local pastor.

No trace of administration or curriculum is found, but it appears that the school was patterned after the schools of Denmark.

NYSTED FOLK SCHOOL[1]
Nysted, Nebraska

Early History.—The folk school in America which had the most humble beginning was that of Nysted. It began in 1887 in an old, unused grocery store, with Reverend C. J. Skovgaard as its director, and two assistants. Soon a building was erected by local interest. On the day of dedication the representative of the local Danish colony, which was one of the largest in America, expressed the hope that the school might be a Danish-American school using the English language and teaching agriculture. The school, however, remained Danish until the last decade when the hope expressed in 1887 became a reality, but then it was too late.

In 1891 a corporation, "Højskoleselskab," was formed to pay the debt of the school. When this was accomplished, the corporation gave the school to the new director, H. C. Strandskov, who came from Ashland High School. This gave the director full authority in matter of administration, policy and curriculum.

The Staff.—As a rule the staff consisted of men and women who, like the directors, had been educated in Denmark, most of them at the famous Askov Enlarged Højskole. Some of the teachers were educated in theological seminaries and after a period of teaching returned to Denmark. Some of the teachers knew little of the English language or of American conditions.

The Students.—At the beginning the students were young men and women who had come from Denmark and wished to learn English. The winter term was for men and lasted five months, while the summer term was for women and lasted only three months. As im-

---

[1] Rev. Hans Hansen, Dannebrog, Nebraska, started a Folk High School near Nysted in 1884 which had fair attendance during the winter months for a few years.

migration gradually stopped, American born young men and women came to comprise the student body. Their ages averaged between 18 and 25, while those from Denmark averaged slightly higher. The school was partly co-educational as women were often admitted to the winter term.

Curriculum.—Concerning the courses, Reverend Aage Møller, the last director, writes: "The subject matter used was the Bible, literature, history, sagas, folk-lore. It would not be wrong to say that in so many ways they portrayed the laws of the spirit, personal sacrifice, beauty, truth. Their view-point was not of the utilitarian kind."[1]

Speaking of the impression which these subjects made upon the students, Reverend Møller continues: "Most of the students look back on their attendance as the one unique experience of their lives."[2]

Influence.—Considerable influence has gone out from Nysted High School to many homes and communities. Many of the former students have become leaders in farm organizations, cooperatives, educational societies, and churches.

To the Nysted colony the school meant the intellectual, social, and cultural center of all that was good. The people looked to the teachers for leadership in all kinds of enterprises. The colony and the school were thus closely knit together for a common good.

The Situation in 1934.—With the economic depression of 1929, and the drought of the Middle West, Nysted High School faced grave financial difficulties. The people who formerly supported the school were unable to do so any longer. Furthermore, the American born students preferred the accredited state high schools and colleges.[3] Nysted High School had failed to American-

---

[1] From a personal letter to the writer.

[2] "Ibid."

[3] Nysted High School was not accredited.

ize sufficiently to satisfy the American born youth. Therefore, the school, which had been a success for so many years and had had an enrollment of about 60 students a year, was forced to discontinue operation in 1934.

The last director, Reverend Aage Møller, who still lives at the school, has expressed the hope that as soon as conditions are favorable, Nysted High School will be reopened, although some reconstruction might have to be made.[1]

DANEBOD FOLK SCHOOL
Tyler, Minnesota

Motto: "An Education Not for Learning but for Life."

Early History.—In 1885 the Danish Lutheran Church of America bought the preferred right to 35,000 acres of land in Lincoln County, Minnesota. In the spring of the following year the first settlement by Danish immigrants was made, and in June of that year the Danish Lutheran Church of Tyler was organized. Immigration continued to increase so that by 1888 the settlement called its first pastor, Reverend H. J. Pedersen of Ashland, Michigan. This was a fortunate choice as Reverend Pedersen was much interested in the Folk High School movement.

In 1888, Reverend Pedersen was instrumental in having a building erected large enough to serve as his home and as a dormitory and classroom for 20 students. This was the beginning of Danebod Folk School. An invitation was sent out for the winter course for 1888-89 with the result that the new school could open with about

---

[1] From a personal letter to the writer, July, 1938.

20 young men. This small but satisfactory beginning marked the establishment of one of the most successful folk schools in America.

For a period of 13 years Danebod Folk School was directed by the able founder, Reverend Pedersen. When he resigned in 1902, he was followed by a fully as able folk school leader, Reverend Thorvald Knudsen, who developed the school to an extent equalled by no other folk school in America.

Enlargement.—In 1917 the main building which served as dormitory and classroom was destroyed by fire. A new spacious brick building was erected with accommodations for about a hundred students. The $33,000 which the building cost, was raised by the Tyler and other Danish-American communities. Other buildings now in existence are the gymnasium, a cottage, and a general assembly hall.

School Term and Source of Students.—Until 1931 the regular school terms for young men have been from December 1 to March 15; for young women from May 1 to August 1 of each year. Although most of the students have come from the local community, there have been students from other communities in Minnesota, from Iowa, North and South Dakota, Montana, Nebraska, Wisconsin, and even from states as distant as California and New York. In 1931, due to financial depression, the director found it advisable to discontinue the winter term for young men, but to maintain the summer term for young women. During the summer of 1934 the enrollment was 62. This arrangement is only temporary and the winter term will be continued as soon as financially possible.

Student Expenses.—The cost of attending Danebod Folk School is $10.00 per week for tuition, board, and room. The State Department of Education in Minnesota has shown considerable interest in the work of the folk school and has made an appropriation of funds to needy students who are residents of Minnesota.

Students: Education and Life.—Danebod Folk School is for adults between the ages of 18 and 25 and for young men and women of all nationalities. The course for women is for two summers. Some of the students have been graduated from the state high school, but most of them come from the farm community with very little education beyond the eighth grade. What they wish is a general enlightenment and appreciation of things cultural and social, and such an opportunity Danebod Folk School offers, as the following paragraphs written by Marietta Strandskov, the director's wife, will show:

"Again we invited young women to share a summer of activity with us. Each term has been so different from the previous, so characterized by the participating group, that we quite naturally are wondering what this summer will be like. Where do your interests lie? What will you have to share with us and how much will you share? There are so many opportunities before us; every day offers a new chance for growth. Let us make use of it and "use our steam through the cylinder in the day time and not waste it through the whistle at night."

"Many are the activities here; most of them depending upon your interests and desires, and with your cooperation we shall spend many a delightful hour singing, dramatizing, arching, tennis playing, hiking, embroidering, etc., not to mention programs and parties.

"Here at Danebod we also have a regular course of studies, but I would rather call these courses, literature, lectures, devotions, and Bible hours, periods of fellowships. These periods we never miss without good reason, and during these hours many do experience a sense of real fellowship that is never forgotten. But I should also like to cultivate a few skills. I believe it is Albert Schweitzer who maintains that a person who can read and write, but is entirely devoid of any manual skill, is a rather useless member of any civilization. Perhaps the Mexicans have glimpsed something of this, since in their public schools the children spend the first years learning the art of pottery-making, while conversing on many subjects. After that, time enough for the three R's. Denmark, frequently spoken of as one of the most civilized countries, ranks manual skills very high; witness their needlework, weaving, lace-making, cabinet work, etc.

"So we shall endeavor to develop skills, tastes, and appreciation of all that is beautiful. It is impossible to draw interest until we have made an investment."[1]

The Staff.—The teaching staff consists of the director and his wife and seven teachers. The director and his family and most of the teachers live in apartments in the dormitory. The teachers eat, play, and associate with the students. The school is a little community of friends interested in the same thoughts—the betterment of themselves and their country.

Influence: National, Community, Individual.—Each year during the last week of June, Danebod Folk School conducts an "International Week." Men and women of various national groups—Danish, Swedish, Norwegian, Polish, Ukrainian, Indian, German, French—are invited to interpret cultural values from their national background. Such a program is a fine recognition of the contributions made by other nations to the evolving American culture. It is an expression of the cooperative spirit so dominant in the life of the Danes for almost a century.

This, however, is not the only contribution made by Danebod Folk School, for the present director, Holger Strandskov, writes:

"Naturally the Danebod Folk School has served not only as a center of interest for the young people, but also as a social center for the people of the community as a whole. The custom was established from the beginning and has been carried out through the many years, that at least one evening a week is regarded as "Open House" at the school. On these evening the farmers come from the farms, the people from town, and young and old share an evening together. Often the main lecture rooms and adjoining classrooms will be filled to the utmost capacity. After an opening song or two, the lead-

[1] Danebod Folk School Bulletin, Tyler, Minnesota, 1936.

er of the school or one of the assisting teachers, or at
times a visiting speaker, will then give the evening lecture. This may deal with literary or historical subjects,
some phase of our social relationship, or an evaluation or
appreciation of drama or music. A number of songs will
again be sung by the audience. Possibly some individual
or a student choir will now render a musical selection.
Afterward all will retire to the student dining room
where coffee and lunch will be served. Here another
short hour is spent as various groups share in conversation. The subject of the evening speaker may be discussed further by a small group or possibly by the group
as a whole.

"The influence of the folk school has given to the people of the community an appreciation of music, song,
drama and physical culture."[1]

Such community education is possible when an institution maintains the ideals contained in the following
excerpt from "An Invitation" by the director to the
summer students of 1936:

"Life is in itself a gift. Every day, yes, every moment
we live is filled with an endless invitation to accept the
real values of life. So often we close our eyes and our
ears to this invitation. Each such refusal is a link in the
tragic realities of the ultimate refrain: It might have
been!

"N. F. S. Grundtvig of Denmark is regarded as one of
the finest interpreters of the life philosophy of the folk
school. He refers to this invitation of life by saying:
'Youth is not a period of mere preparation for later deeds.
It is the great period of decision, the turning point of
life, when purpose and will are generated, when the
young man or woman must gather spiritual impetus for
the long race before him.'

"Thus the folk school extends its invitation to youth
to share the real values of life, the human values, as revealed in the song of the poet, the living saga of man,
and not least in friendship and fellowship.

"We are at this time inviting young girls to share with
us at the Danebod Folk School through a period of eight
weeks. Our type of school has never emphasized the
necessity of a definite curriculum for the student. The
main emphasis has been that the subject dealt with in a
lecture or a class period must of necessity be interpreted
by personality through the living word."[2]

[1] "Ibid.," pp. 5-6.
[2] "Ibid.," pp. 7-8.

Since 1888, Danebod Folk School has aided many young men and women to see and realize the values of life through the influence of one personality upon another. Numerous letters from former students speak of the full life they can enjoy because they have attended a cultural school like Danebod where the everyday things of life are of the greatest concern.

An Estimate by a Student.—The following letter, written by a student of non-Scandinavian parentage, gives an excellent estimate and interpretation of the folk school:

"The doors of Danebod are about to fling open and the halls will again echo with 'Welcome' and happy song.

"At this time I wish to express my sincere appreciation to Reverend Holger Strandskov for accepting a stranger into the student body, and for giving me the privilege of returning this year.

"I would also like to take this opportunity of expressing my thoughts about the Danish Folk School, and perhaps answering a few questions, put to me so frequently, particularly by Americans.

"The first question asked is: 'Why did you go to Danebod?'

"Every story has a beginning! The early years of the 'Depression' found me in a financial world, an eye witness to the parade of 'broken lives.' The laborers came first and one shall never forget the look in their eyes as realization dawned upon them that the relief line was imminent; it was also sad to watch the 'white-collar' workers follow with their dreams of security completely destroyed.

"Stepping out of that chaotic world, the writer stepped into another, that of social service. Here again, the parade of 'broken lives' continued, and it became evident that there was no solution to many of the problems, other than in education.

"We have proof of this, in the important emphasis which is now being placed upon adult education. Because of this new emphasis, many individuals, as well as certain institutions, (particularly during the last two years) rushed forward with the banner: 'We are the parents of Adult Education' only to discover that adult education has been with us in one form or another since Adam experimented in teaching the first born.

"We know, however, that the eyes of leaders in adult education are focused on the Danish Folk School movement; it was, therefore, in quest of observing the apparently successful methods and feeling that after all, material gifts count but little.

"I soon discovered the true meaning of the words, 'An Education not for Learning but for Living.' There was no such thing as standing on the side-lines and observing; one immediately became initiated into the program of activities. The students accepted me into their midst and made me promise to pay nickels to the 'Pig' for breaking laws made by themselves.

"Time will not permit for a complete reviewing of the program, but I enjoyed every minute. The day began with a lifting of thought to God and Song . . . singing continued throughout the day.

"I was particularly impressed with the idealistic spirit which prevailed in the gymnasium—here was none of the heated excitement of competitive games, but a complete blending of unity and harmony, and genuine fun. Gymnastics form a very definite part of the Danish Folk School; apparently Denmark is more interested in the development of healthy bodies than "beating the other fellow.'

"The afternoon coffee was an enjoyable feature of the program, and the lectures which followed were like a bouquet of flowers. Each lecture had a distinctive style, and the variety was endless. Music, singing, games, folk dancing, moonlight walks, firelight programs, and Sunday picnics contributed toward our social life.

"I was delighted with the informality of the school. In the beginning, it was rather shocking to hear dignified professors called by their first names, but later it seemed quite natural. It was also fun to watch distinguished guests join the kitchen line to wash their own 'afternoon coffee cups.' The Danish people are free of class consciousness.

"One of the fundamental philosophies of the Danish Folk School is that of sharing and cooperation, and I saw a very fine demonstration of it during the summer term, not only between the students, but the faculty and members of the community.

"Leaders of the Danish Folk School refer to it as a 'School of Thought'—it is their hope that those who enter may find something therein for all life. In my own case, I forgot that I came to study methods and techniques and my experience has been far richer. I like to think of Danebod in terms of a fountain of clear water from which one may drink and feel refreshed.

"I am grateful for the summer of 1935 and am looking forward to the summer of 1936, with many thanks."[1]

---

[1] "Ibid.," pp. 14-17.

This tribute is a recognition to the many friends of Danebod who through their gifts made it possible for this and many other young women (the average age is about 20) to receive an education that made life worth living and to the teachers who pointed to ideals in life which can be attained through constructive thinking and hard work.

Financial Problems.—As has already been pointed out, Danebod Folk School has accomplished much through the years. Of the many problems it has had to deal with, the financial has been the most difficult. From the very beginning it lacked the funds with which to realize the ideals of its founder. The men who supported the school in 1888 have died, and new supporters have failed to take their places. The uncertainty of private gifts has hindered progress more than anything else.

Thus today the school conducts only the summer session for young women from May 1 to August 1.

Lack of continual and sufficient financial support has also affected the equipment, the enlargement of the library, the hiring of more and better teachers, the efficiency of the teachers, and the advertising of the school. Although face to face with these serious problems, the present director, Holger Strandskov, plans to reopen the winter term for young men from December 1 to March 15. The director feels a personal responsibility in helping youth, especially the farm youth, to a better understanding of themselves and their places in the world of thought and things.

ANSGAR COLLEGE
Hutchinson, Minnesota

The Beginning of a College.—In the winter of 1901 the Danish Lutheran College Extension Association was organized for the purpose of erecting a college in the large Danish settlement in and around Hutchinson, Minnesota. The organization was incorporated with a capital stock of $50,000. This stock was sold in $50 shares. Much interest was shown in the undertaking. Two Americans donated each ten acres of valuable land to the Association.

In 1902 a stone structure was erected with accomodation for 214 students. The chapel had a seating capacity of 700. This new institution, named after Ansgar, the Apostle to the North, opened in the fall of the same year with a staff of 20 teachers and almost 200 students.

The Great Disaster.—But in February, 1903, the very first year of its existence, the main building burned at a loss of $30,000. With the insurance money ($22,000) and a few private gifts, a new building was erected and opened for use in the fall of 1903. Although the school opened again with 20 teachers and more students than the year before, the financial loss was too great to overcome, and as a result Ansgar College was sold in 1904 to an American company which converted it into a business college.

A Typical People's College.—The success which this short-lived Danish college met showed an interest in the type of training a school based upon the ideas of Grundtvig and Kold offers. Ansgar College, even though it included many academic courses and methods in its curriculum to accommodate some of the students in the vicinity, adhered nevertheless to the historical lecture method of teaching, maintained the Danish Folk School life and spirit, and stressed personal guidance.

The "Might Have Been."—It is difficult to estimate what this institution might have meant to the State of Minnesota, but it can safely be said that it would have taken its place with other influential institutions of higher learning, had it received financial support.

LUTHER COLLEGE
Racine, Wisconsin

Decision to Build.—Racine has the largest Danish population of any city in America. Many Danish church conventions have been held in that city. At one of those conventions held at the beginning of this century the United Danish Lutheran church in America encouraged the building of a school patterned after the Danish Folk High School.

Favorable Location.—A corporation was formed and a beautiful place on a hill overlooking the city of Racine was chosen for the erection of a college. In the midst of these fine surroundings, the cornerstone was laid on July 4, 1902, and the building ready to dedicate October 31, 1902.

Luther College opened with a fair enrollment. Most of the students were from Denmark or of Danish parentage. This institution existed only a short time. From available information it appears that the failure was due to lack of financial support. The United Danish Lutheran church owned a college in Blair, Nebraska, and did not feel able to support two schools. Accordingly Luther College was closed and the building sold.

BRORSON HIGH SCHOOL
Kenmare, North Dakota

In 1905 the North Dakota District of the United Danish Lutheran Church built a high school in a large Danish settlement near Kenmare, North Dakota. This school named after the famous hymn writer, Bishop H. A. Brorson, and located on the wide prairie of the North, played an important part in the cultural and spiritual development of the settlement. The school was under the able leadership of Jens Dixen, an untutored but intelligent lay preacher, who labored faithfully for two years as its director and then went to Australia and New Zealand as a missionary, soon to return again. He spent the summer doing manual labor and the winter conducting school.

Almost all of the students came from the immediate vicinity. The courses were mainly academic and served the settlement as a regular high school. Special afternoon and evening lectures and discussions were conducted weekly.

Due to lack of financial support the school existed only about fifteen years, but it helped to educate young men and women who later became leaders in state and church affairs.

ATTERDAG COLLEGE
Solvang, California

A Folk School on the Pacific Coast.—The first attempt to bring the Folk School movement to the Pacific Coast was made by Reverend Benedict Nordentoft when he, in 1911, built a school in the new Danish colony at Solvang, California. The school was welcomed by all the Danes on the Pacific Coast, and there appeared to be a bright future for this new institution. In less than two years the buildings and equipment were found inadequate. The local community and friends of the director from near and far came to the assistance with funds for a new building large enough to accommodate at least 50 young men and women.

Co-educational.—The school from the beginning was co-educational and had students coming from all parts of the United States. Many came to spend the winter in California and attended the regular term which lasted five months.

Director.—Reverend Nordentoft was director and owner of Atterdag College and accordingly had a free hand in all matters of administration, curriculum, and student activities. He received support from various sources, such as students in attendance, private individuals, most of them former students of other folk high schools, and from friends in Denmark. Some support was also received from the Danish Lutheran Church of America.

Publications.—Each year a catalog was published to describe the purpose of the school, its activities, and its program.

Curriculum.—The curriculum resembled that of the average Folk High School in Denmark. The subjects were entirely of a cultural nature—intellectual and physical. History and Danish constituted the main subjects, but art, literature, sociology, and English, received much attention. The free lecture method was employed and textbooks were omitted wherever possible. To take the place of textbooks, subjects of the survey type were frequently assigned for the purpose of acquainting the students with books and available information.

Students.—A school with an attractive location like Atterdag College surrounded by unusual natural beauty would, of course, draw students from all parts of America. These students, generally about sixty in number and between the ages of 20 and 30, were all of Danish parentage, many of them having been born in Denmark. A few of the students were high school graduates, but the great majority had only an eighth grade education and several years of experience in manual work. Some of the students came from the city, while most of them came from the farm, and practically all returned to their former work.

At Atterdag College, as in other folk high schools in America, physical culture was emphasized and held a prominent place in the life of the school. As a rule the Swedish and Danish methods of gymnastics prevailed. One hour a day was given to instruction and practice of physical culture.

The Staff.—The director as well as the teachers have all been Danes. This was necessary since Danish was used in classroom and at social activities. Most of them were college graduates or graduates of theological seminaries. The director has always been a minister who often served the local congregation and travelled extensively on behalf of the college.

Three directors have served Atterdag College since it was organized in 1911. These are:

1911-1921..Rev. Benedict Nordentoft; now in Denmark
1921-1931..Rev. Ewald Kristensen; now in Denmark
1931-1937..Rev. Marius Krog

The Present Situation.—The writer has been authoritatively informed that at present Atterdag College has no director, and it is doubtful that it will have one, at least as long as Danish is maintained as the official and prevailing language in classroom and in social activities. The demand for retaining the Danish language is made by the Danish colony at Solvang which now controls the institution. It is the wish of the colony to have Atterdag College as a community center of Danish language, literature, and art—or in fact, a Danish cultural center.

The Failure to Make Adjustment.—Atterdag College enjoyed success for a quarter of a century under fine leadership, but it failed to adapt itself to the conditions of America, or rather it failed to Americanize. Immigration stopped and the children of Danish-American parents were sent to state high schools and colleges. This hindered the progress of Atterdag College. It was found that the second generation did not understand or appreciate Danish as the parents did. The children demanded English and an accredited school. Atterdag College failed to give either, and as a result was forced to discontinue.

Reasons for the Failure of the Folk High Schools

A casual observer might view the record of the Danish Folk High Schools in America with misunderstanding unless all the facts involved are considered. In an analysis of the reasons for the failures we shall find that the causes were of such a nature as to be beyond the control of the director in almost all instances. Let us briefly observe some of these general causes.

During the discussion of each Danish folk high school the **financial problem** has been observed to be the main cause for the short existence of most of the schools. Too many of the schools depended upon support from friends. The enthusiasm aroused among friends at the beginning did not last. When drought, economic depression, or local disagreements occurred, support dwindled to practically nothing. In no instance did the writer find definite arrangements for sufficient and dependable support.

The financial situation might have been remedied if a thorough **survey** had been made previous to the establishment of a folk high school. Hardly ever was a survey made to find out whether sufficient interest and demand existed, and if the Danish population was large enough to support a folk school. The schools were generally the creation of a strong personality.

Another serious difficulty was that of the scattered population of Danes. There are in America about 500,000 Danes of whom about 200,000 were born in Denmark. But this population is scattered over the entire country and naturally makes concentrated school work difficult. A thorough survey would, of course, have revealed this situation.

In every instance the **director** had too many duties. He was responsible for getting support for the school, for the policies of the school, for getting students, and had to teach an average of ten hours a week. He was generally the pastor of the local congregation. Besides this he was expected to, and did, travel extensively. In some cases he was editor of a weekly paper. Despite the versatility of the directors they were unable properly to administer all duties.

Practically all of the directors and teachers in the folk high school before the year 1900 had been exclusively educated in Denmark. Some of them were called directly from Denmark to be directors of schools in America. Concerning this, one director, Kristian Oster-gaard, who came to Elkhorn High School about 1880, wrote several years later:

" We moved to America with the Danish folk high
school. But America was, and continued to be for many
years, a strange land to us. In thought and sentiment we
lived in Denmark, and in all that was Danish. The inner
life of America we knew nothing about or perhaps we
were beginning to discover it from the distance. This
was a mistake which often found expression in unfortunate judgments of that which is American."[1]

Since few of the **teachers** had degrees, the schools
were not accredited and in addition did not have sufficient funds to meet the requirements for accrediting.
Until the World War the students were from Denmark
and did not wish credits for their work. However, during the war the students came from Danish-American
homes with a desire for credits. About 1927, immigration began to cease and there was no longer a demand
for learning English at the folk high schools. This
brought about an acute situation with few students
wishing to avail themselves of that type of education.

As already intimated the **folk high schools failed** in
most cases **to Americanize.** They remained Danish within a community which was rapidly becoming American.
Many a Danish colony expected the folk high school to
keep the Danish language alive for them, while they
themselves failed to support the school with students
and money. It may justly be said that Nysted and Danebod High Schools succeeded because they desired to
make their contribution in the English language. Even
as late as 1937, Atterdag College was closed because the
Danes in the immediate vicinity refused to permit a
change from the Danish to the English language in the
school. The opinion prevails there and in many other
Danish communities that the cultural contribution of
Denmark can only be made through the Danish
language.

[1] "Danske i Amerika, Vol. I, p. 333.

Summary.—In conclusion we might make some general inference regarding the folk high schools.

The schools as a rule are located in the country or small community.

The schools are owned either by the director or a corporation.

The administration and policy are intrusted to the director.

Most of the teachers have part, if not all, of their education from advanced folk high schools in Denmark.

The schools have a winter term of five months for men and a summer term of three months for women. A few are co-educational.

The students come largely from the farm and are between the ages of 18 and 25.

The schools are not accredited and give no credits or diplomas.

Support of schools has come from various sources, mainly from private gifts and student fees. Student fees have as a rule been very low.

The general aim has been and still is to help young men and women to know themselves and their talents, their God and life's values. Closely connected with this aim is that of perpetuating Danish culture and language.

Hundreds of students look back with joy and gratitude upon the term or two spent at a folk high school. They realize the influence which it had upon their lives. But the influence also extended beyond the student body into the surrounding community. To the community the folk school was generally considered the intellectual, cultural, and social center, and in a few instances, the religious center.

CHAPTER VIII

AMERICAN FOLK SCHOOLS

America is known as a country of educational experiments. Many valuable experiments have been made which have led to the improvement of our educational system and the systems in other parts of the world. Among these experiments the Folk High School, which originated in Denmark in 1844, has had its share. In 1885 the Agricultural College of the University of Wisconsin began an experiment with farm youth some of whom had not even graduated from the grade school. The curriculum, methods of teaching, discipline, and general student activities appears to have been based upon the Danish Folk School, only with minor changes to fit local and American conditions. As will be observed later in this chapter, the experiment has been a great success with more than 6,000 students bearing witness to this fact.[1]

This same success has been experienced by Walsh County Agricultural and Training School at Park River, North Dakota. This school, the first of its kind in the State of North Dakota, was started through the efforts of A. S. Gibbons, a man of Danish parentage and a state senator. Since its establishment in 1913 it has helped thousands of young men and women to be happy and progressive tillers of the soil.

---

[1] The writer has interviewed a number of former students of Farm Short Course and heard only favorable expressions.

A folk school, which has alrealy made a worthy contribution to the people in the mountain area of North Carolina, was started by Mrs. John C. Campbell in Brasstown, North Carolina, in 1925. This experiment has turned out to be of immense value to the adults in the vicinity. The school has been active in folk education, in establishing cooperatives, and in general farm enlightenment.

In the following pages the story of the above three schools will be considered. The writer as far as possible has avoided interpreting in order to let the facts speak for themselves. All three schools are strictly American in spirit.

THE FARM FOLK SCHOOL [1]
College of Agriculture

Early Beginning.—In 1885 a group of interested farm leaders in the State of Wisconsin desiring to prepare the farm youth for the problems in agriculture conceived a plan of a Farm Short Course based upon the Folk School of Denmark. Those leaders, acquainted with some of the agricultural problems of Denmark during 1870-80 and the manner in which the Folk Schools had dealt with the problems, saw great possibilities for such educational institutions in Wisconsin. The time, however, was not quite ripe for the development of an educational institution which offered no credits, no degree, and no diploma at the end of the course. The school, therefore, began with a few students, but it was a beginning. The number of students gradually increased as the young men returned to their respective farm communities to advertise and show the

---

[1] A similar school is connected with the University of Minnesota and operated on the same plan. The cost of attendance for three months is about $80.00.

value of a winter short course for young farmers. By 1932 no less than 5092 boys had attended the Farm Short Course which is connected with the college of agriculture of the University of Wisconsin.

The Farm School since 1932.—In 1932, Dr. Chris L. Christensen, Dean of the College of Agriculture at the University of Wisconsin, became interested in the educational needs of young farmers, and made special efforts to reorganize this Farm Short Course into a Farm Folk School. Dr. Christensen had visited Denmark and was interested in helping the Wisconsin farmers to a better understanding of their agricultural and economic problems. He therefore organized what is now called the Farm Folk School, including many of the ideas and principles of the famous Folk Schools of Denmark.

Administration.—The Farm Folk School is under the direct supervision and leadership of the Dean of the College of Agriculture of the University of Wisconsin. The teaching staff is a part of the College of Agriculture and is paid by the University. The Farm Folk School, by being part of the College of Agriculture, is enjoying the advantages of trained and experienced agriculturists and economists, and the students have an opportunity to hear many national and foreign leaders in agriculture.

Curriculum.—The courses are for two winter terms, four months each. Most of the students stay two winters and a few have come back for a third winter. The purpose of the course is expressed in the following paragraphs by Dean Chris. L. Christensen:

"The welfare of Wisconsin depends to a great extent upon the condition of its farming, the economic and social state of its rural communities, and the prosperity and progress of the farmer. For many years men trained in the Short Course have been contributing to **agricultural** leadership. Today the College of Agriculture, through this four months' winter Farm Folk School, is making available to young men on farms a broad cultural training for rural leadership as well as technical training in the agricultural sciences. The new Farm Short Course trains in civic problems and farming."[1]

The Folk School includes many practical and technical subjects. These subjects are to meet the demands of the students from every county in the State of Wisconsin.

Students.—There has been a steady increase in the number of students attending the Farm Folk School. In 1937-38 the number reached 350. These boys come primarily from the farm and return to the farm. Many of them are high school graduates while others have finished only the grades. There are no entrance requirements and the students need not pass any examinations at the end of the term. The requirement is that they have had at least two years of practical experience on a farm and are in the age groups from 19 to 25. A few are older.

Cost of Attending.—The Farm Folk School is financially within the reach of a large number of farm boys. The cost is as follows for a period of 15 weeks:

```
Room ($1 a week) ................$15.00
Board ($4 a week) ................ 60.00
Fees (Laboratory, infirmary)....... 22.00
```

The Regents of the University of Wisconsin offer 20 scholarships of $75 each to the first-year students who are residents of Wisconsin. A business concern offers 15 scholarships of $45 each.

Credits and Certificates.—The student who attends two winters and secures 36 credits with a mark of 60 or more receives a certificate. If he has a grade of 85 or more and wishes to enter the University for a degree

---

[1] Bulletin of the University of Wisconsin, The Farm Short Course, April, 1935.

he will receive full recognition for all the courses taken in the Farm Folk School Course.

Extra Activities.—A simple and informal lecture method is used. The students have few textbooks and assignments, but references are made to books, magazines, and farm publications available in the University Library. Three or four evenings a week the young men meet for the "evening forum." At these meetings the students have an opportunity to hear and discuss current economic and social problems with leaders from both off and on the University Campus. During the winter of 1937-38 the discussion dealt with health, industry, labor, insurance, education, art, transportation, economics, foreign trade, cooperatives and many other subjects of interest.

Working Together.—Learning to work together forms an essential part of the Farm Folk School. In the classroom the students rub shoulders, they all eat together in the dining room and all sleep in the same dormitory. The rooms, although well heated and lighted, are simply furnished. The dining room is on a cooperative basis. Thus the students learn cooperation by doing.

Influences.—The writer interviewed a number of men who had been students at the Farm Folk School. Those interviews might be summarized in a few inclusive statements. The Farm Short Course has created great interest in farming on economic and scientific basis, interest in keeping order on the farm, interest in cooperatives and in working together for a common cause, interest in community affairs and in leadership, and interest in production, distribution, consumption, and prices of products. During the 52 years in which the Farm Short Course has been in existence no less than 6,629 trained farm youth have gone into every county

of Wisconsin. Since 1932 more than 1500 students have
been trained to take their place in the farm community.
What this has meant to the progress of agriculture in
the State of Wisconsin no one is able fully to estimate.
That the Farm Short Course has been and still is a
mighty power for good, no one can deny. The men who
have attended the Farm Short Course are satisfied and
progressive farmers improving agricultural America.

At the close of an interview, Dr. Chris. L. Christensen, Dean of the College of Agriculture at the University of Wisconsin and director of the Farm Folk
School, said to the writer: "As I see the success of the
Folk School students, I am becoming more and more
convinced that the Folk School movement has a great
future in America. Our school is one attempt to help
the generally neglected farm youth and the experiment
has been so successful that we have to turn students
away for lack of accommodations. I am sure the Folk
School would be a success in other ways than agriculture."

WALSH COUNTY AGRICULTURAL AND TRAINING SCHOOL
Park River, North Dakota

Motto: "Hand and Brain."

Although the school about to be described is not strictly a Folk High School, there are sufficient resemblances
to the Danish schools to warrant its recording in this
chapter. In fact, the founders had the Folk Schools in
view when Walsh County School was organized.

**The First School of its Kind in the State of North
Dakota.**[1]—In 1911 State Senator A. S. Gibbons intro-

---

[1] Benson County Agricultural School at Maddock, N. Dak., was built
in 1914.

duced into the legislature of North Dakota a provision which called for the establishment of two Agricultural Schools, if the counties that voted to have them would assume half the financial responsibility. This act, called the Gibbons Act, was passed in 1911. The following year, Walsh county voted to have the one and Benson county the other. A petition was presented to the Board of Commissioners of Walsh county in September, 1912. The proposition voted upon at the November election of 1912 was favorably passed with an appropriation of $13,000.

The Location.—The people of Park River had taken the initiative in establishing the school and it was only natural that the school should be located in their community. A drive for raising funds was made with the result that by January, 1913, the citizens of Park River had donated $1,600.00 with which to purchase a site for the building. Further appropriations to the extent of $35,000.00 were made by Walsh county. The building was put into use in the fall of 1913 but was not finished until 1914. The building was surrounded by rich soil, favorable for experimentation.

Publications.—The first announcement of the School was sent out in July, 1913, by the principal, W. A. Broyles. Since then, regular bulletins and a high school paper, "The Wildcat," have been published.

Administration.—The control of the School is intrusted to a Board of Trustees consisting of five members of whom three must be farmers and one the county superintendent of schools. There are two advisory members —the President of the Agricultural College at Fargo and the State Superintendent of Public Instruction.

Purpose.—In the first annual catalog published in

1914 the following purpose is set forth for Walsh County
Agricultural and Training School:

"It is the purpose of the Agricultural and Training
School to offer a course which shall make students want
to stay in school instead of dropping out of school. The
elimination of students from school at the age when they
most need schooling has been no less a determining factor in the growth of the county school movement than
the demand for better agricultural training. The purpose of the school will be as far as possible to give the
students an opportunity to grow and to develop into
competent citizens. Tillers of the soil need the latest
agricultural knowledge, so that they may be enabled to
meet changing conditions and to make farming pay without absorbing all their thoughts and energies. A part of
the attention of successful men and women must be
directed to their relations with their neighbors, their
families and to the nation and state. Good roads, good
schools, good churches cannot be kept up by untrained
citizenship. The general culture of students in the Agricultural and Training School is given much attention.
The idea is summed up in the school motto, 'Hand and
Brain.'

"Aside from the instructional life of the school, the
institution is a center for agricultural discussion. The increasing number of calls that come from farmers of that
county for milk or grain testing or for advice in scientific matters is a source of gratification to school authorities and teachers. The third idea of the county
school is the training of rural teachers. Young men and
women should be encouraged to teach near their homes.
They should be trained to think that good training is
essential, not that just anybody can teach a country
school. The Agricultural School offers an excellent
teachers' training course. Instruction in agriculture, shop
work, and domestic science is given to all students in the
course. The purpose of this course is to develop
teachers with the proper viewpoint toward rural life
and with sufficient training to enforce their ideas."[1]

Twenty years later, the following statement regarding the objectives of the School were summarized in
"The Wildcat," the student paper:

"The Walsh county school was started and has been
administered with these purposes in mind:
To make young people stay in school.

---

[1] Walsh County Agricultural and Training School, First Annual Catalogue, 1914, p. 21, 22.

To train those who will inherit or own land.

To inspire respect for honest labor and for book learning.

To give the farm boy and the farm girl special individual attention.

To furnish a school with institutional atmosphere and individuality where students and patrons may feel at home.

To give another chance to those students whose early education has been neglected.

To train teachers in sympathetic understanding of rural problems so that they may be especially fitted for rural teaching .

To supply a center for the agricultural discussion of the county, and to add dignity to farm labor.

To work with rural teachers as a part of the same school system.

To help in creating for rural life a background of culture and an understanding that will make it what it should be—the happiest career obtainable."[1]

The Staff.—The superintendent (formerly designated principal) has general supervision of the school and is responsible to the Board of Trustees. He is chosen by the Board of Trustees. The teachers in turn are responsible to the superintendent. In matters of policy and student activities, they act as an advisory board.

The Students.—So far, the school has received its largest number of students from Walsh county, although practically every county in the State of North Dakota and several states in the Union have been represented in the student body. Most of the students are between the ages of 15 and 20, with some past 20.

Attendance.—From the first year the school has been well attended except for a short period during and after the World War. The following table of figures shows the attendance from 1918 to 1936:

---

[1] "The Wildcat," student paper of Wash County Agriculture and Training School, 1933.

Period	Students
1918-1919	45
1923-1924	126
1928-1929	227
1933-1934	304
1935-1936	308

This remarkable increase is made yet more commendable in view of the present employment of former students of the school.

Occupation	Percentage
Living on farms	82%
Teaching rural schools	7%
In business	4%
Students	4%
Miscellaneous	3%

It is quite obvious that the Walsh County school has succeeded well in doing what it proposed to do—teach the farm youth to stay on the farm.

The Curriculum.—The nature and content of the curriculum has no doubt influenced a large percentage to stay on the farm. The courses which especially contribute to farm education are those listed under the heading of Agriculture. To satisfy general demands Walsh County school offers courses in Agriculture, General, Home Economics, and Commercial subjects. These courses are all in the **Long Term High School Course** which begins in September and ends in May. The courses under the heading of Agriculture, for the four years, are as follows:

First Year	Second Year
Mathematics I	English II
Soils and Crops	General History
Farm Shop	Types and Breeds of Livestock
English	Feeds and Feeding
Citizenship	Biology
Project Work	Project Work

Third Year	Fourth Year
English III	Farm Management
Farm Machinery	and Marketing
Plant and Animal Disease	Problems of American Democ.
Poultry and Horticulture	Adv. Arithmetic
Elective	Business English
Business Law	Elective
U. S. History	English IV

Walsh County School offers also a **Special Winter Short Course** which generally lasts from about November 15th to March 15th. This course serves the young men and women who do not have time or means to take the Long Term High School Course. Many of the students attending this course are between the ages of 20 and 30, and some are older.

The Special Winter Short Course is for three years and is divided into four parts: Agriculture, Mechanic Arts, Home Economics, Commercial. The subjects listed under Agriculture are:

First Year	(Second Year, continued)
Farm Crops and Soils	Drafting of Farm Buildings
Spelling and Penmanship	Farm Carpentry
Arithmetic	Adv. Engineering and
Forging and Gas Engines	Blacksmithing
Electricity	
Carpentry	Third Year
	Farm Arithmetic
Second Year	Rural Economics and Sociology
Business English	Farm Management
Business Law	Marketing of Farm Products
Feeds and Feeding	Animal and Plant Diseases
Breeds and Judging	and Pests
of Livestock	Farm Machinery and Farm
Mechanical Drawing and	Mechanics

From the above quoted course it appears that there is a mixture of academic, technical, and practical subjects. The Long Term High School Course seems to be mainly academic, while the Special Winter School Course is more practical and technical.

Academic Standing.—Walsh County School is fully accredited by the North Central Association of Accredited Schools and Colleges and also a member of the National Honor Society of Secondary Schools. Students completing the Long Term High School Course are eligible to enter any college or university.

Entrance Requirements.—Students who have completed the eighth grade or its equivalent are admitted to all courses. Students who have not completed the eighth grade, but who are at least sixteen years old, are admitted to the agricultural or domestic science courses if they seem to the superintendent to be able to do the work.

Students receive credits for equivalent work done at other schools if the subjects for which credits are asked are the same as those taught in this school. The students will be admitted with advanced standing upon presentation of a certificate showing that they have completed a required amount of work in other schools.

Any student of sufficient maturity may be admitted to the short course, regardless of academic preparation. The short course is especially suited to young men and women who are older than the usual students or who cannot afford to attend the whole term.

Sources of Income.—Where does Walsh County School receive its support? From the beginning the **State** has contributed toward the maintainance of the School. At present the sum is $7,500. This is based on enrollment. The guarantee is $5,000 if the enrollment is 150 or a fraction thereof. For each 100 more students or a fraction thereof the aid increases by $1,000. Walsh county contributes an equal amount which at present is $7,500.

Room and Board.—Dormitories or private homes are provided for the girls and boys who live outside of

Park River. The dining room is run on a cooperative basis. Many of the students receive food from home and do their own cooking. The cash expense for such students is about $50.00 for the Short Course. The cost for room and board is about $16.00 a month. Books and incidentals amount to about $6.00 per year.

Student Activities.—The activities are well balanced to give all students an opportunity for expression. The activities include plays, operettas, physical training for boys and girls, basketball, band, football, Home Economics Club, and the Future Farmers' Chapter.

Contributions.—In the course of the description of Walsh County Agricultural and Training School we have already observed some contributions made by this new experiment in secondary education. For the sake of clearness and brevity we shall list the specific and general contributions.

It has helped young people to stay in school.

About 90 per cent of the students have remained on the farm.

Knowledge of farming has brought satisfaction and prosperity to hundreds of farm homes.

The School has dignified farming.

Farm leadership has been produced.

Cooperation forms an integral part of the entire school and has shown itself in the communities where former students reside.

During six weeks of evening meetings, farmers, old and young, come from far and near to hear lectures on soil conservation, farm finances, how to raise wheat, and various types of livestock. This is a great contribution made by the School to Walsh County. The present

Superintendent, E. J. Taintor, said to the writer: "I believe our school is making an important contribution to the farmers of Walsh County and to the State of North Dakota. The bankers and business houses of Park River **know** who the farmers are that have attended our school."

JOHN C. CAMPBELL FOLK SCHOOL
Brasstown, North Carolina

Motto: "I Sing Behind the Plough."

"A folk school is a large family circle, the ties being spiritual rather than physical, where all are keenly interested in the world about them, in their origin and in their destiny; a group where all work for the common good by developing the best powers they possess, and giving the circle the full benefit of their efforts."[1]

The Founding of an American Folk School.—The above quotation is a description of the life at the John C. Campbell Folk School at Brasstown, North Carolina, founded by Americans in a non-Danish community. The school was organized in the fall of 1925 and named after the late John C. Campbell, Director of the Southern Highland Division of the Russell Sage Foundation and author of "The Southern Highlander and His Homeland." Mr. Campbell gave his entire life and energy to better the living conditions for the mountain people of the South. He considered the Folk School the best means to reach this noble end.

Location.—The school is located in the extreme southwestern mountain corner of North Carolina. It is in Cherokee county where there are great possibilities for agricultural development. This favorable situation was combined with a desire on the part of the citizens themselves to have "a school which would build up the coun-

---

[1] Fred C. N. Hedebol, "Cooperation," January ,1933.

try and not make just preachers and teachers."[1] "The
desirability and feasibility of rural cooperation form
the basic premise upon which the school was founded.
It has therefore deliberately made itself a part of the
life of the community in which it is situated, so that its
program is of concern to the entire neighborhood during the entire year. Its activities fall into two main
groups; a course for young adults, inspired by the Folk
School of Denmark, and a wide variety of community
undertakings—recreational, cultural, educational, and
economic."[2]

Ownership and Responsibility.—The school is owned
by a Corporation with Mrs. Olive D. Campbell as the
director. The director has final authority although
technically limited by the Board of Directors which
consists of four men and six women. In practice the
Board of Directors considers itself advisory rather than
assuming any authority. In fact, the director and the
staff exercise as little final authority as possible. In
matters requiring important decisions the director of
the school consults the staff and then the Board of Directors. Each staff member is responsible for his or her
phase of the work, the director advising and questioning rather than assuming final responsibility. Besides
the staff and the Board of Directors there is an Advisory Committee consisting of nine men and two
women.

Sources of Income.—The income for the school is
from private gifts, with the exception of about $2,000
given by the Board of National Missions of the Pres-
byterian church and the American Missionary Association of the Congregational church. Like most of the

---

[1] Leaflet published by Director Olive D. Campbell, Brasstown, North
Carolina.
[2] "Ibid."

Folk Schools in Denmark, the farm and the industries connected with the school contribute much to the funds needed for general expenses. The yearly income from the school, farm, and industries, amounts to about $40,000.00.

Yearly Publications.—As a rule the school issues two leaflets a year—partly as a report on the progress of the work and partly for the purpose of raising funds.

Teaching Program.—The courses taught are largely determined by the character and interest of staff activities. "For example, the farm manager teaches agriculture as well as singing games. The dietitian teaches crafts, etc. The purely cultural subjects such as history, geography, English, arithmetic, etc., are taught by those who have a special interest in the knowledge of them. The teaching is very closely tied into the life and experience of the section. It is largely discussion or a very informal lecture in method, or in actual doing. Textbooks are not used, but reference is made to books available, and effort made to interest students in reading. There are no examinations or credits."[1]

The Teaching Staff.—The personnel consists of twelve teachers, including the dietitian. There are two in the farm department, three in the craft department, one secretary, and one forester-architect-builder. The subject taught is closely connected with the work assigned each teacher. Since the school is not accredited, little stress is laid on academic training. The necessary courses for general enlightenment, such as history, literature, and aritmetic are offered each year. Only the English language is used as the school is strictly American and has no relation with Denmark or anything that is Danish, except in spirit.

---

[1] Quoted from a Personal letter to the writer.

Students: Ages, types, education.—The school is co-educational and generally there are a few more girls than boys. With few exceptions the students are between the ages of 18 and 26 with the average age as 21. Speaking of these students, Mrs. Olive D. Campbell, the Director, writes:

> "They are young people from the mountain section and almost entirely from the farm. The length of the course is four months (November 1 to March 1), but as almost everybody works his way and as many stay during the spring and summer to help with the farm, dairy, garden, canning, etc., they often stay a year. Students staying a second year usually specialize in the very practical departments in which we are able to use them and give them training. A few repeat the regular course, which is never the same from year to year. Most of the young men have done some farm work and often have worked in forest industries, trucking, and some have been in 'public works' such as mills, woodworking plants, etc. The girls have usually not been away from home. Some of the students, after their term here, go on into fields of special instruction, short courses, etc., and a few go on to college."[1]

The amount of education which these students have had before coming to the Folk School varies considerably. Many are high school graduates while several have had only a seventh grade education and some have had still less. The purpose of the Folk School is not to supplement the public school or to give academic training but

> "to give the young people new horizons, new interests, new ideals, which will enable them to live a richer life in the surroundings to which they were born. The course of instruction is so planned that, if it makes the young men and women aware of deficiencies in their community, it also shows them the tremendous possibilities of rural life and indicates the method by which it may be dignified to the point of becoming interesting, profitable, and even thrilling to those who live on the soil."[2]

Accomplishments and Influences.—So far, we have observed the purpose and general working of this new

---

[1] "Ibid."

[2] A leaflet written by Mrs. Olive D. Campbell.

venture in rural adult education, the Folk School. A natural question which follows such a discussion is this: What has the John C. Campbell Folk School actually accomplished? Although the school is as yet young some definite and admirable accomplishments have been made:

Since the Folk School was organized in 1925 an area of 125 square miles has been influenced in the matter of general enlightenment—culturally and agriculturally.

In 1935 seven per cent of the Brasstown community was on relief as compared with 25 per cent in the neighboring Cherokee communities and 34 per cent in Clay county.[1]

No less than 600 farmers covering an area of 125 square miles have organized the Mountain Valley Cooperative. This Cooperative handles the various dairy and poultry products, feeds and seeds, and other farm necessities. The Cooperative also operates a corn mill. The board of the Cooperative consists of members from the staff of the Folk School and of the community.

Likewise, members of the staff and of the community serve on the board of the Brasstown Credit Union. This Union provides a means of community saving and makes small loans for constructive purposes.

In regard to the social side, **"Men's and Women's Clubs** widen the circle around the school center and work for all that goes to enrich the life of the community and section."[2]

"Crafts, which enjoy ever-growing favor with the local people, give satisfaction to the creative power and help to supplement farm income. A carver is no longer an idle whittler; he is a craftsman and a financial asset.[3]

[1] "Ibid."
[2] "Ibid."
[3] "Ibid."

It is rather difficult to analyze these accomplishments for the purpose of finding the reasons for such a success. However, some general reasons might be stated, such as the personalities directing the entire Folk School in all its relations, a thorough study and understanding of the social and economic needs of the section, friendly relation with the rural population, and practical as well as purely cultural activities. The two most important reasons for the success are undoubtedly the first two, namely—leadership and understanding of local conditions and needs.

Conclusion.—In 1935 a visitor from the State University of North Carolina said: "I wish every county in North Carolina had a school like this."[1] To which the Director answered: "We wish so indeed. Economic relief is not enough in itself, nor good schools, nor social measures of one sort or another. Every country section needs some kind of enlivening center which will interpret, stimulate, radiate, cooperate, live life as it might be lived under existing conditions. Such a center may show certain tangible results in a few years, but its real influence will not be clear for a generation or more."[2]

To the above schools might be added two of recent date, showing the continued attempts made to establish folk schools in America.

THE NORTH DAKOTA FARM FOLK SCHOOL
Fargo, North Dakota

The North Dakota Farm Folk School was started November 15, 1937, with an enrollment of four students for the first five weeks. The following program was

---

[1] Leaflet, John C. Campbell Folk School, April, 1935.
[2] "Ibid."

offered: General Assembly, Soil Management and Conservation, Farm Shop, Livestock Production and Management, The Cooperative Movement, Farm Literature and Farm Correspondence, Farm Business, Farm Gardening, and Parliamentary Practice and Community Activities. Before the first five weeks' term expired, seventeen more young men had joined the courses.

Throughout the period from the beginning of the enterprise, a systematic campaign of publicity was carried on through the press and the radio, in order to make the public conscious of the fact that a new type of Agricultural Education was being made available. The general interest evinced and the general public approbation, led the school to issue the first twenty-four page illustrated Farm Folk School catalogue, which described in detail, some fifty proposed courses, for the winter term of 1938-1939.

The original program for the Farm Folk School at the North Dakota Agricultural College, was first presented to the State Board of Administration in the fall of 1938. The State Commissioner of Agriculture and Labor, together with another member of the board, expressed great interest in the folk school education and instructed Dean H. L. Walster of the Agricultural College to submit a request for $5,000 with which to develop a Folk School Course. The request was approved and the school was to have three terms of five weeks each. In the fall of 1938, the National Youth Administration established the Resident Training Work Project in connection with the Farm Folk School. The school was authorized to borrow $12,000 with which to purchase building material for the project, this sum to be returned by rent of rooms. Two unused Army Corps Barracks on the Agricultural College Campus, were remodeled to provide room for sixty students and classrooms. This project increased the student enrollment to seventy-four.

The students came from twenty-six counties in the State of North Dakota. Besides the Folk School Course, the N.Y.A. students were required to work seventeen and one-half hours a week on the project. Special evening sessions were held for the various purposes. A special course on "First Aid" was offered by the Works Progress Administration Instructor.

Student Attitude: The attitude of the majority of the students has been favorable. No particular attempt was made to enforce rigid attendance rules, since it was felt that the strength of the enterprise rests primarily upon the awakening of interests and enthusiasm, rather than in regimentation. It was found necessary, however, to exercise greater rigidity in attendance rules.

In **student government,** an attempt has been made to make the residents of the Farm Folk School realize that they are adults with personal responsibilities. Most of them have responded favorably. The **teachers** of the North Dakota Agricultural College assisted in various capacities in the Folk School Course. Some additions were made to the staff of the Folk School. The method employed in teaching is the lecture method. Individual student participation in each class exercise has been stressed. A coordinated program involving several subjects, seems to be favorable, depending upon the objectives of the Farm Folk School instruction.

The average youth of eighteen to twenty-three years of age is interested in the mechanical aspects of farming. There is no doubt that the Farm School enrolees have shown greater interest, and have worked more faithfully at those courses where they have had to use their hands. However, there is a danger of over-emphasizing this purely vocational aspect of instruction.

The most difficult task of the Farm Folk School is to secure qualified teachers for those aspects of interest which involve men's relationship with his fellows—the social, economic, governmental, and business relationships. "Here too, the methods of instruction must definitely get away from traditional lecturing, because that is deadening, uninspiring, and passive as far as the student is concerned," said Dean Walster to the writer.

The tuition for each five weeks' term is seven dollars and fifty cents. One dollar is charged for medical examination and service. The room rent amounts to one dollar per week.

Without doubt, this farm school has a future in the great farm state of North Dakota. It might be wished that this school was located in a farm community, in the middle of the state. It is likely, however, that many such schools will be established in the future in the State of North Dakota as there is a general demand for farm education among the rural people.

THE FARMERS UNION FOLK SCHOOL
Jamestown, North Dakota

For a number of years many of the members and leaders of the North Dakota Farmers Union have realized the need of farm education. These men and women saw that the high schools spread over the state and the eight professional schools for higher education did not offer what the majority of the population of this great farm state needed. North Dakota contributes more professionally trained young men and women to other states than any other state in the Union, because North Dakota does not have sufficient professional positions available for its graduates.

This situation and the need of an intelligent farm population brought a group of farm leaders together in 1934. These men and women represented thousands of farmers who were interested in the same thing, namely, farm education. The plans for a school were made on the basis of need and not standards. Credits and examinations were considered immaterial; minimum cost was to be maintained so as to prevent no one from attending. The entire school was to be a cooperative enterprise and self-supporting.

The Farmers Union School opened in February, 1935, in a warehouse in Jamestown. At once it attracted a number of students from various parts of the state, many of whom were destined to be leaders in their own communities. In 1939 a hundred young men and women between the ages of 16 and 35 attended the six weeks of school. They were interested in their work, the improvement of themselves and their social and material standing. They were also interested in improving the conditions of their fellow men. To this noble and timely aim many of them pledged themselves unselfishly and whole-heartedly.

The Farmers Union School is conducted informally with stress on cooperative living and common responsibility. Open forums and discussions of pertinent questions are a part of the daily schedule. The evenings are devoted to lectures by leaders who are outstanding in their field. These lectures are usually followed by general discussion. The courses taught deal with farm management, agricultural subjects, markets, public speaking, writing, practical arithmetic, economics, and social science.

The teachers are men and women interested in the betterment of farm youth and farm conditions. Some of them are college graduates with degrees, while others have had much practical experience on the farm and in business. The present director is Mary Jo Uphoff.

Plans are being made and funds collected for a permanent folk school to be called "The Talbott Memorial." With a permanent school and teaching staff several school terms can be conducted during the year. This school is destined to become a great influence upon the farm population of North Dakota. It is one more effort to prove that the ideas of Grundtvig and Kold do work on American soil.

CONCLUSION

In the discussion of these American Folk Schools located in various parts of the country we notice great success. These schools have succeeded because they were carefully planned, and are on strict business basis; they had financial security; they used the English language and applied the Folk School principles to American conditions. It might be said of the founders that they were practical realists and educators, who understood human needs and local conditions.

It is interesting to observe that the Folk Schools started by Americans have all been successful and are steadily growing, while the schools started by Danes in Danish communities have with few exceptions all failed. The reasons for the failures were listed in the previous chapter.

It appears quite obvious that if a Folk School is to amount to anything it must adopt American ways, have financial security, and accept students of all nationalities.

CHAPTER IX

FOLK SCHOOLS IN EUROPEAN COUNTRIES

Since the first folk high schools were organized, visitors from all parts of the world have travelled to Denmark to see how these private, unpretentious, and non-accredited schools, working with farm youth having only an eighth grade education, could change the status of a country from national disaster to national victory. How could these peasant schools make such great contributions as community education, scientific farming, and a cooperative system which now includes 90 per cent of the rural population and 5,000 societies doing business to the extent of $250,000,000.00 per year?

Some educators have spent months studying these folk schools and left, still wondering how they could make such contributions, while others have been inspired to establish similar schools in their countries.

It is the purpose of this chapter to briefly state the extent to which the folk schools have been adopted in other European countries.

I. The Folk Schools of Norway

The men who in 1864 introduced the folk schools in Norway had been students in Denmark. Ole Vig, teacher and editor, took the initiative in advocating a movement for general enlightenment. The work of establishing a folk school was done by Herman Anker and Olaus Arvesen. They erected the first school at Hamar. This school as well as all the schools established in Norway resemble the Danish schools in administration, location, curriculum, age of students, and contributions.

Many of the leading men of Norway looked with suspicion on the new folk school movement because it was closely connected with the Grundtvigian religious movement and because it favored "Landsmaalet," a language based upon common dialects of Norway; and because it competed with the county high schools (Amtsskoler) which were established in 1875. Despite this opposition, the folk schools of Norway now number more than 30 with a yearly attendance of about 2,000 students.

In the year 1900 a better understanding was brought about between the folk schools and the county schools, which were much alike. The minister of education had discovered after a survey that the county high schools did not succeed in keeping their students on the farm as well as the folk high schools. This discovery gave equal rights to both schools in regard to state aid. Aid was also given to needy folk school students. Today, the Norwegian folk high schools enjoy the same privileges as the Danish.

Grimley describes the folk schools of Norway in 1937 in the following words:

> The students must be at least 17 years old. The purpose is to teach the students to seek information independently and learn to think for themselves. Hardly any textbooks are used. Much of the teaching consists of lectures and free discussions. They delve freely into literature with discussions on the ideals of its men of genius. The currents of history—past and present—are discussed.

> The folk school movement in Norway started in the sixties of the last century and is, therefore, now about 70 years old. It has exerted a tremendous influence on the cultural development in the valleys of Norway. It has stressed the national values and the public spirit. It is now, as before, primarily the country population that attends these schools. They are all supported by public means and their work must be approved by the Department of Education.[1]

---

[1] Grimley, "The New Norway," p. 152.

II. The Folk Schools in Finland

Finland is known as a "land of singing." When Dr. Elias Lonnrot collected the Finnish folk songs into what is called "The Kalevala" and J. L. Runeberg wrote "Fanrik Stals Sagner," the Finnish people sang the folk schools into being. Singing is a part of the folk school movement.

It was Uno Cygnaeus, the father of sloyd, who had travelled widely, who became the spokesman for the folk school movement. But it was a woman, Sofia Hagman, who, in 1889, organized the first folk high school at Kongasala near Tammerfors. She had been a student at Askov Folk High School and had visited Sweden and Norway to study their schools. She gathered a group of girls and taught them handwork and some cultural courses such as world history, literature, geography, and drawing.

In 1891, Borga Folk School was organized. The same year a school, Kroneby High School, was organized and resembled in almost every respect the Danish and Swedish schools. The funds for this school were nearly all collected by the university students at Helsingfors.

At first the State granted no aid to the folk schools but in 1907 an agreement was made that the schools should have regular aid direct from the State. This has been helpful for the schools as they now number about 50 with one-third using the Swedish language. The great influence of these schools has been general enlightenment and the development of a highly organized cooperative system which includes all of Finland.

III. Swedish Folk Schools

During the middle of the eighteenth century Sweden was in much the same national and spiritual condition as its neighboring country, Denmark. A spirit of indifference prevailed in the rural population with the result that few were interested in the welfare of the country.

It was under such conditions that a nobleman, Grev Torsten Rudenschold, laid the foundation for general enlightenment. But it was Dr. August Sohlman, editor of the daily, "Aftonbladet," in Stockholm, who protested against materialism and at the same time brought the need of new schools for farm youth before the people. Dr. Sohlman had served in the Danish army in 1864 and had at the same time visited at the Danish schools. After his return to Sweden he sent one of his editorial assistants to Denmark to make a thorough study of the Danish folk schools. A series of articles on the work and influence of the Danish schools appeared in "Aftonbladet." Some of the articles were contributed by Danish folk school leaders.

This campaign, started in 1867, led to the establishment of three schools the following year. Dr. O. V. Aalund, the man Sohlman had sent to Denmark, became the first director of the first folk school at Herrestad. The second school was started by Dr. C. A. Bergman at Onnestad and the third school by Dr. L. P. Holmstrom at Hvilan.

Sweden has now more than half a hundred folk schools scattered throughout the country with an average yearly attendance of about 4,000 students.

The Swedish folk schools are like the Danish in ownership, location, administration, student activities, and influence. In method of teaching and in curriculum the Swedish schools are more formal and academic than the

Danish. The director, usually called "Rektor," generally has a doctor of philosophy degree. Most of the teachers are university trained men and women.

A deviation from the Danish schools is found in the combination of two schools, the folk school and agriculture school, into one school called folk school. Each school has its own dean, but one director for both. A year at a folk school department is required before entering the agriculture department. The students generally attend two terms.

To agriculture and to rural culture and life the folk schools have been a mighty force in the re-making of Sweden. Wherever the folk schools have come, their cooperative enterprises have flourished. Therefore what Mr. Childs says of Denmark might well apply to Sweden: "The metamorphosis that occurred in Denmark in the half century from 1880 to 1930 is nothing short of miraculous."[1]

IV.   The Influence of Danish Folk Schools in England

In 1888, David M. Lewis of Wales was studying at Goteborg, Sweden, where he heard a lecture on the Folk High Schools in Denmark. He later wrote for the lecture and had it published in the "Journal of Education" in 1890.

In 1894 Director Alfred Paulsen from Ryslinge was invited to deliver a series of lectures at Oxford University on the subject, "The Danish Folk High Schools." Director Paulsen stressed the practical significance which the schools have had for the economic development of the rural community. This impressed the English people.

A few years later J. S. Thornton visited Denmark and was much impressed with the work of the Danish schools. In 1901 he made a special report to the British government.

Speaking of Denmark, Bishop Dr. I. Perzival said in an address at the University of Wales in 1900: "This has been a great wonder for us Englishmen (referring to the agricultural development of Denmark), while we ourselves, suffering the same agricultural depression, have done nothing but complain about our unfortunate circumstances."[2]

The Bishop further observes that "of the chairmen of dairy organizations, 65 per cent, and of the managers of dairies no less than 90 per cent have been students of Folk High Schools." He then asks: "How long shall we in England wait for similar results?"[3]

In 1900, and again in 1903, a group of Englishmen visited the Folk Schools of Denmark. It was especially Frederiksborg Folk High School which inspired the English to have a school of their own. The famous historian, Holger Begtrup, was the director. He had told the English party that 80 per cent of leaders in cooperatives were former folk school students. This interested them as the English had many cooperatives.

In 1909, Tom Bryan established the Folk School on English soil at Bournville, near Birmingham. About 1912, Jonty Hanaghan, after a two-year stay at Frederiksborg, returned to begin a school at Yorkshire. Continual exchange of students and teachers took place between these schools and Frederiksborg.

The Folk High School movement never prospered in England. There are three reasons for this:

---

[1] Childs, "Sweden the Middle Way," p. 133.
[2] Schrøder, L. Den Nordiske Folkehøjskole, p. 463.
[3] "Ibid.," p. 464.

The heroic spirit of the past had been awakened by the English poets before the ideas of Grundtvig reached England.

Cooperatives were well established in England long before the first Folk School in England was built (1909).

England enjoyed political, religious, and personal liberties to a greater extent than Denmark.

There has been in recent years considerable interest in adult education growing out of the Folk School movement. But this type of education has lost so many of the Folk School features that it can hardly be considered here.

V. Influence of Danish Folk Schools in Germany

A number of noted German educators visited the Folk Schools of Denmark between 1885 and 1900. Some of the visitors were Superintendent Kaftan of Kiel, Director Conradi from Hohenwestedt in Holstein, and Principal Fr. Lembke from Heide. These men wrote favorable comments in German newspapers and magazines about their findings.

About 1890, Dr. Maikki Friberg (Helsingfors) lectured on the Scandinavian Folk Schools in various parts of Germany. In 1897 she received her doctor of philosophy degree from the University of Zurich on the thesis "Entstehung und Entwickelung der Volkshochschulen in den nordischen Landern. Her lectures created considerable interest.[1]

During the Social Congress in Berlin in 1890 the Danish representative, C. F. Tietgen, had a lengthy conversation with the German Emperor, Wilhelm II, about the Danish Folk High Schools. The following year he visited Denmark and discussed the schools with Tietgen. Nothing, however, was done in Germany.

---

[1] Schrøder, L., "Den Nordiske Folkehøjskole," p. 466.

A few years later a noted German scholar, A. H. Holl-
mann, visited Askov Højskole and other schools and
made a thorough study of the Folk High School movement from its beginning. His findings are written in
"Die Volkshochschule."[1] This book is commonly considered the best account and interpretation ever written
of the Danish Folk High School. This masterpiece created considerable interest in the movement but the attempts did not meet with success. What was the reason
for this?

Since the War of 1864 the relation between Germany
and Denmark has been somewhat strained at times. Although the Germans won the war, there has been among
the German people a hesitancy to adopt anything Danish. This is the underlying reason why no Folk High
School succeeded anywhere in Germany. Some time
after the War of 1864 Rødding Folkehøjskole was reopened but the school was Danish and was closed after
considerable opposition.

But the philosophy of Grundtvig rooted in love for
God, home, work, and native land, has not been lost
entirely. The writer, after three visits to Germany in
1936-1937, discovered much in the modern educational
movements in Germany that can be traced directly to the
ideas of Grundtvig and Kold. For example in the book-
let, "German Education Today," written by Theodor
Wilhelm and Gerhard Graefe,[2] we read:

> The achievements of the young manual worker are
> placed on the same level as those of the brain-worker.
> This recognition of the dignity and nobility of every
> honourable achievement proves to young Germany that
> it is the worker and not the capitalist who guides the
> destiny of the nation, that the important factor is, not
> money, but creative achievement.

---

[1] Published by Terramore Office, Berlin, 1936, p. 19.
[2] "Ibid."

We quote further:

> The young long for finite values. They long for the teacher to speak to them from his heart and to stretch out his guiding hand. John and Nietzsche attacked most vigorously the intellect and the cult of book learning.[1]

Since the time knowledge of the Danish Folk Schools came to Germany, special agricultural schools have been developed. These schools resembling clearly the Danish, have been of much interest to Hitler.

In the following quotation we find a description of these schools:

> The technical continuation school of agriculture is the education centre for the German peasant. It gives peasants and farmers the opportunity of deepening and extending by a one-year course the practical and theoretical knowledge they already possess. Their chief object is to strengthen the peasant's feeling of attachment to his native soil and to intensify his sense of national solidarity.
>
> To be admitted to such an institution a pupil must prove that he has had a good general education, corresponding to the intermediate certificate. In addition every pupil must have reached at least his twentieth year and must show that he has three and one-half years' practical experience of agriculture. The total number of students at such an agricultural school must not exceed 50. [2]

VI. Influence in Iceland

The People's College movement has also spread to Iceland. There are several schools working more or less according to the plan and in the spirit of the Danish People's Colleges. They have been established in rural communities and have contributed considerably to the general culture of the people; in particular toward strengthened national feeling and stronger sense of independence.

---

[1] Published by Terramore Office, Berlin, 1936, p. 5.
[2] "Ibid.," p. 16.

CHAPTER X

THE APPLICATION

A liberal education is truly and fully useful, though it be not a professional education. Though the useful is not always good, the good is always useful. Good is not only good, but reproductive of good . . . .

An intellectual man, as the world conceives him, is one who is full of "views" on all subjects of philosophy, on all matters of the day.

—CARDINAL NEWMAN.

In the first chapter some of the problems in American education were discussed, and rather severe criticism was directed against the professional, the technical, and the academic types of education offered alike to all the country's young people. Some of the dangers and unfortunate results growing out of such a system of mass education were briefly pointed out.

Later the discussion centered on the People's College as it has been developed and applied in Denmark. Although this type of school has no academic standards, and its program and methods are difficult to state in terms of definitions, it has, nevertheless, proved to the world for three-quarters of a century that cultural education is the most profitable for the rural people of Denmark.

Then were considered the three great contributions of the People's Colleges. These are community education, scientific farming, and cooperatives. The remarkable progress made by the Danish farmer was attributed to the influence of these cultural centers.

In the three previous chapters were observed the work of the People's Colleges in other countries. As for America, we noticed that the schools started by Danes maintaining the Danish language were not very successful, while the schools organized by Americans have met considerable success. This would tend to prove, then, that some of the principles of the People's College when Americanized can be applied to America. But these American schools have been agricultural schools stressing the practical and technical rather than the cultural. The interest of this book is in the cultural side of the People's College.

The question considered is: can some of the ideas on cultural education which have proved successful in the People's College of Denmark apply to American conditions, or are the racial, social, economic, and agricultural differences of such a nature that no application can be made?

Hegland, at the close of his bulletin, says regarding the People's Colleges:

> Judging by the service which they have performed in Denmark and other countries in the direction of cultural, economic, civic, social, and religious advancement, it would seem that these people's schools have an especially significant contribution to a native living under a government of, by, and for the people.[1]

In speaking of the work and the success of the People's Colleges, Hart says:

> There is here only an actual recognition of the supreme problem of our present civilization: the critical understanding of the fact that there can be no change in our civilization save as that change takes place on the inside of civilization, and on the inside of individuals, groups, institutions, communities; and the setting forth of a method which has been found effective in a little—but great—people of Europe and which, by implication, might be found equally effective, if intelligently adapted to our changed conditions in American life.[2]

---

[1] Hegland, "The Danish People's High School," p. 165.
[2] Hart, "Light from the North," pp. 155-156.

These educators believe that there is a possibility of applying some of the ideas, principles, and methods of the People's College to American conditions. The system may have to undergo some changes to fit the conditions of America, and yet, fundamentally the means and the end will not differ greatly. America is, of course, a very large country compared with Denmark. Its population is heterogeneous, representing practically every nation on earth, as compared with Denmark's homogeneous nation in which eighty-five per cent of the population is of the same nationality. America has a new culture which is still in the making, as compared with the old traditions and culture of Denmark. America is a nation with practically every type of farming as compared with the two types of farming in Denmark— cattle and grain raising and dairying.

Although these great differences do exist, it must be admitted that the agricultural problems in Denmark are not essentially at variance with those in the greater part of America. Furthermore, the teaching in the People's Colleges is not merely applied to one type of farming but rather to an intelligent participation and application of the individual to whatever problem is confronted. This type of teaching is fully in accord with Grundtvig's philosophy and psychology of universal principles. The problem of application to American agriculture offers, therefore, no particular obstacles. It is to the farm community in particular that the People's Colleges have made their contribution, although the influence has gone farther. Differences in size of country, type of people, and culture are of minor importance in the application. The program of the People's College is sufficiently elastic to fit our rural conditions in America.

Apparently there is in America a need for **community**

interest in youth. Everywhere communities must be awakened to a realization of the problems that youth faces today. Parents often unite in deploring the fact that their sons and daughters are idly wasting their precious, formative years on the streets. Occasionally the parents expect the church to take the lead in providing every kind of desirable amusement; but the church is not a state institution, and all the inhabitants of a single community seldom belong to the same church and many do not belong to any church at all. The problem, then, belongs to the community, and unless there is more community consciousness and a greater feeling of responsibility for youth, there can be no solution.

What the community is, its youth will be. Grundtvig realized this in his educational work. As shown previously, the Danish community is an educational center in which youth with profit can spend the intervening four years between grade school and the People's College. Those years of activities in the community serve as an excellent basis for cultural studies.

A community awake to the problems of youth will try to solve the **leisure problem** by providing good and wholesome recreation. This may be in the direction of a community library and reading room, lecture and music organization, good plays, Boy Scouts, baseball, basketball, 4-H clubs, and other worthwhile recreation and enterprises. In all activities the parents should show an interest that would result in the best possible recreation. The interest of the parents in recreation means much to young people.

Fittingly does Hart say:

> Education is not apart from life: it is just the adult generation giving its own world to the new generation. And be sure that adult generation will not give a very different world from that in which itself lives. The adult generation cannot keep its own private evils, tra-

ditions, greeds, autocracies, shame, follies and insincerities, and ask the school, working in the midst of these effective influences, to produce a new generation committed to good, to science, to altruism, to democracy, to honesty, to wisdom, and to sincerity. The democratic problem in education is not primarily a problem of training children: it is the problem of **making a community** intelligent, disciplined to freedom, share in the tasks of the age. A school cannot produce this result: nothing but a community can do so.[1]

Closely connected with community interest in youth should be its interest in common work. At the time of Grundtvig, youth wanted an education that would take them away from the common tasks. Grundtvig raised the value of ordinary work so that youth came to love his work on the farm or in the shop. He has learned to sing as he goes about the daily task:

> I am just a simple farmer,
> Downright and plain,
> And yet I love my modest calling,
> For around my little home
> Grow blossoms fair
> With color and perfume.
> Mine is the clear spring,
> Mine is the fresh breeze.[2]

A community awake to problems is also awake to the value of work and better education. Europeans once considered America a nation where hard work was man's closest companion. The author has observed a decided change in the European attitude during his ten years of absence. Now they regard America as a country of idle men. This European attitude would make little difference if it were not for the fact that since 1928 a change has taken place in America. At that time federal and state relief and welfare work was hardly known except in congested, poor districts of large cities, although such aid should no doubt have been given even in small communities. Ten years later

[1] Hart, "Light from the North, p. XIV.
[2] "Folkehøjskolens Sangbog."

(1938), however, there are states where almost half of the population is on relief. For this unfortunate situation, the economic depression and drought are generally blamed. Although the depression and drought have caused untold financial, physical, and mental suffering, there is still another contributing factor which is often overlooked, namely, the attitude toward **work**. The pioneer spirit of self-initiative in trying new things has decreased.

Following the World War, prices on commodities were high and new machinery gradually replaced human hands. To many, living became easy. Little by little some began to think of life as all play and all leisure. When in 1929 the economic depression set in, some men no longer had the desire to do hard work. This is undoubtedly one of the reasons why some Americans are suffering today. It would be well, therefore, to heed the admonition of Gladstone, when he says:

> Try and reconcile your mind thoroughly to the idea that this world, if we would be well and do well in it, is a world of **work** and not of idleness. This idea will, when heartily embraced, become like a part of yourself, and you will feel that you would on no account have it torn from you.[1]

When the implication of the words of Gladstone have been fulfilled in the individual, a new day will have dawned for America, or rather a return to the days of pioneering will have been accomplished. The common worker will say with Carlyle:

> For there is a perennial nobleness, and even sacredness, in work. Were he never so benighted, forgetful of his high calling, there is always hope in a man that actually and earnestly works: in idleness alone is there perpetual despair. Work, never so mammonish, mean, is in communication with nature; the real desire to get work done will itself lead one more and more to truth, to nature's appointments and regulations, which are truth. The latest Gospel in this world is, "Know thy work

---

[1] Gladstone, "Correspondence," Vol. 1, p. 160.

and do it." "Know thyself." Long enough has that poor self of thine tormented thee! thou wilt never get to "know" it, I believe! Think it not thy business, this of knowing thyself; thou art an unknowable individual; know what thou canst work at, and work at it, like a Hercules. That will be thy better plan.[1]

A School With a New Philosophy of Education

Having thus created community interest in youth and their welfare as well as a wholesome attitude toward common work, the road is prepared for the establishment of an institution with such underlying principles as those of the Danish People's College. Hollman, the German scholar has in his book, "Die Volkshochschule," given an excellent interpretation of the Danish schools. In the introduction he writes:

These schools are called high schools because they deal with things of high concern in the life of the community; and they are called People's High Schools because they are related to the whole life of the people and to those things, only, which are important to all the people. Their aim is the creation of a popular national culture which will ramify out into whatever special interest may be found in human nature, but which in its fundamentals is homogeneous and the possession of all. The path to this goal is by way of the education of personality; only through the inner freedom of personality can such a culture develop.

In order to secure this high sense of common living, the individual must be freed from the stifling constraints of the mass; he must come to know himself as a self-directing person. Therefore inner freedom is the highest law of these schools; they do not breed submission or regimentation of spirit, but they teach the comradeship of all in the life of the community. In a word, the spirit **of these schools is the spirit of democracy.** It stands, therefore, in opposition to both the current popular opinion of our times and to that doctrine of the over-lordship of the state in the midst of which we have but lately been living and whose form, now broken, lies behind us.

Hence, it is obvious why these schools could not have been accepted, hitherto, in any land where the idea of the supremacy of the state has prevailed; there is no room in such a state for the spirit of these schools. How-

---

[1] Carlyle, "Labor," p. 190.

ever, the less welcome such schools are in an authoritative, magisterial state, the more room there must be for them in a people's state. Otherwise we shall find ourselves presently demonstrating that caricature of democracy of which Herbert Spencer wrote: "New democracy is but old despotism differently spelled!"[1]

An institution with a philosophy of education such as that of the Danish People's College should be able to make some contribution to a democratic nation. Such an institution in America would help to give equal educational opportunities to all. America does not wish to make retrenchments in education. The word "equality," as it was written in the Declaration of Independence, means that all should have an equal opportunity at the task which each individual citizen is capable of doing. With such an interpretation, American youth could look for a new day of opportunities.

In the United States there has been a tendency to minimize the educational problems peculiar to rural communities. The farm youth has his problems about work and education as does the city youth. In recent educational discussions on reorganization of the junior high school and the junior college little recognition has been given to the farm community. Since 30,000,000 persons live in small communities and on the farm, some attention ought to be given to the farm youth whom we expect to raise the farm products in the future. The farm problems are recognized by the federal government.

It was pointed out in Chapter I that the opportunities for a professional education are greater in the United States than anywhere else. To this commendable feature in American education, the writer wishes to see added the opportunities for a general education for farm youth, an education that will meet their problems.

---

[1] Hollman, "The Folk High School," p. V, VI.

Thus far, the farm youth, wishing to receive an education, has had to leave the familiar environment of the country and travel to the city, since almost all of the higher institutions of learning are located in the cities. Separated from the place where his tasks for the future are centered, he spends a year or two in adjusting himself to city conditions and perhaps to fraternity life. For the city youth such surroundings might be conducive to learning, but for the average farm youth it means educating him away from his work and adjusting him to a life he perhaps was not fitted for. As to his future happiness there is considerable uncertainty. The city is not very conducive to the study of farm conditions nor to the making of a future American farmer. It is on the basis of this situation that the writer suggests a new type of school wherein the principles of the Danish People's College, at least in part, could be applied.

The People's Colleges would not take the place of higher education. The young people from the farm, wishing to take up a profession, should not be prevented from entering the university. But the People's Colleges would educate that great number of farm youth which never graduates from high school nor enters the university. As was pointed out in Chapters VII and VIII, the People's Colleges have succeeded well in keeping their students on the farm. And it would not at all be harmful if the People's Colleges received some of the many gifted farm youth that ordinarily come to the university. American agriculture is in need of men with leadership and ability.

Education has done much in the rural districts to break down the European provincialism which the immigrants carry with them to America. But the task has not ended. There are yet communities which are divided into three or four national groups, each having its own language, traditions, churches, and national and religious prejudices. One or two educational centers in a county would greatly assist in melting the prejudices and remove the obstacles to cooperative efforts which are so essential to progress. Such an institution would assist in developing our American culture.

The word culture includes much. The Committee of Social-Economic Goals of America, appointed by the National Education Association, and headed by John Dewey, enumerates the factors that influence our A-merican, evolving culture. The factors are school, language, thought, social life, reading, science, numbers, art, music, social interdependence, truth, demagoguery, civic education, and history.[1] To this list are added the mechanisms of cultures. These are the cinema, the radio, the telephone, and the automobile, the airplane, the telegraph, and the press. The institutions of culture, besides the schools, are the home, the church, the library, the museum, the playground, various clubs and societies, the community government, the state government, and the national government.[2]

The committee concludes with these significant words referring to culture and the philosophy of life:

> What an individual does with his abilities depends upon the interpretation that he puts upon life. It depends upon the answer that he gives to such great questions as: Is there a purpose in the universe? Does this purpose, as it works itself out through nature and in the lives of men, recognize good and evil? Why should I live? Why should I do anything? What will be the outcome of my life?
>
> One's philosophy of life involves one's ideas of morality and religion. As we study the history of the race in story, in biography, and in literature, we "live through and identify ourselves with the finest religious experiences and aspirations of men." We see the struggle of the race to find a clearer understanding of the meaning

---

[1] "Implications of Social-Economic Goals for Education, p. 41-47.
[2] "Ibid.,"p. 47.

of life. The story of human progress includes the growth of mankind in religion, and the study of literature includes the study of the religious masterpieces.

Chapman and Counts say: "In the last analysis science can never tell man what is Beautiful and Good, nor even what is ultimate truth. . . . Generations of scientific inquiry have but added to the mystery of existence. If, in our study of the world of nature, these limitations of science be ever kept before us, instead of appearing to be in conflict with religion, science will but reveal the need for the wider interpretations of life and serve as an indispensable instrument in the realization of human destiny."

The school must help the child to develop his own philosophy of life which gives to human endeavor purpose, vision, inspiration, religion, and morality. They must keep pushing toward the development of an ever widening horizon of intellectual appreciation and a more thoroughgoing consistency with regard to the beliefs which he embraces.[1]

This representative American committee recognizes education as the most important factor in the making of an individual. Education, then, should be of the type that would help man to make the most of life. This is the aim of the People's College, which for almost a century has recognized the importance of culture in education. In recent years considerable recognition has been given to the development of a cultural education in America. But there is yet much to do, as the committee pointed out.

In suggesting a **new institution,** little attention will be given to the administrative side. Such matters belong to local committees; and in the matter of curriculum only broad suggestions are made. Although the State of North Dakota has been kept in mind in planning this, the application might easily be made to other states, with only minor changes to fit local conditions. The fundamental principles would essentially be the same. This is true of the People's Colleges of Denmark, Norway and Sweden.

[1] "Implications of Social-Economic Goals for Education, pp. 49, 50.

Since the State of North Dakota is divided into counties, the boundaries fall conveniently for the establishment of a cultural school. It is generally recognized that many of the small high schools do not have equipment in the matter of books and teachers to offer four years of high school work. These schools could maintain a junior high school and relinquish the last two years in favor of the county school. For more than a century Danish educators have held to the seventh grade as being a favorable age for an introduction to secondary education. In American cities this is generally the division line. But many rural communities will hesitate to accept this arrangement and discontinue the last two years of high school to send their young people to a county **cultural** college. But with an enlightened adult generation, this objection could be removed. The parents would gradually come to realize the value of such an education for their children, as it would keep their children in the county. The two-year course for students above the age of sixteen who wish to finish high school, and the two-year short course of five months each for students eighteen years of age or more, would be given in a community life situation where few new adjustments to conditions would have to be made. In the study of natural and social sciences, applications could profitably be made to local conditions already known to the student. This would tend to give a greater appreciation of local conditions and create a love for home and common work. Having been awakened to such an appreciation of ordinary things, the young man or woman is likely to stay at home.

In every county, provided the population is at least 3,000, there should be at least one cultural school, this school to be conveniently **located** in a central place to make it possible for transportation of a large number of the students and also to give the county full benefit of its influence. Since it is to be in the rural community, to be owned by the people in the county, and to be attended by mature young people, the **name**, People's College, appears to express the true meaning and place of such an institution.

As this institution is to belong to the people and serve their needs, equal representation by all communities is important. The **board of directors** ought, therefore, to consist of one non-political representative from every township or similar civil division in the county. Half of the members on the board should be farmers as this arrangement would tend to give equal and fair representation in the matters of policy and administration, since there would be students from all parts of the county. The state, however, should have representation only in advisory capacity through the Superintendent of Public Instruction.

As was seen in Chapter I, the problem of **support** is a complex and serious one. Remote control is often harmful, since such control might be out of harmony and sympathy with the local needs and the spirit of the institution. To avoid this, the County People's College should be supported equally by township and county. This common share would tend to develop a common interest and responsibility in the matter of youth education. The state might give funds to education in the county, but no requirements should be attached to such funds. This is the policy of the schools and the government of Denmark, as was pointed out in Chapter III. The Danish government has also found it profitable to aid needy students desiring an education. The State and Federal Governments in America might find it to their benefit to assist students who lack funds for education. The Federal Government has helped a num-

12

ber of students through the National Youth Administration, but there is yet much to do in this direction.

In choosing a **director**, great care ought to be exercised. He should be an experienced and a trusted man with a powerful personality. His task should not merely be that of administration and supervision of the school in general, but above all he should serve as an advisor to the students giving them personal guidance in all matters of life. In this most important task he might be assisted by the dean of men and the dean of women. All advice should be frank and sympathetic with consideration for the personal, social, and economic conditions of the student.

The Curriculum

The curriculum offers a serious problem. Some of the students will continue in higher institutions of learning, while the majority will not. But, as Hutchins says:

> Four years spent partly in reading, discussing, and digesting books of such importance would, therefore, contribute equally to preparation for specialized study and to general education of a terminal variety. Certainly four years is none too long for this experience. It is an experience which will, as I have said, serve as a preparation for advanced study and as general education designed to help the student understand the world. It will also develop habits of reading and standards of taste and criticism that will enable the adult, after his formal education is over, to think and act intelligently about the thought and movements of contemporary life. It will help him to share in the intellectual activity of his time.[1]

As the span of human life lengthens and knowledge increases, the years necessary for advanced learning will also increase. Higher learning is becoming more

---

[1] Hutchins, "The Higher Learning in America," p. 81.

and more specialized. The time may soon arrive in which two more years will be added to a university course. The four years at general cultural schools would serve as a valuable foundation for specialization.

The normal life is divided into about three equal parts—leisure, work, and sleep. The last decade has seen the leisure hours become as important as the work hours. Leisure may be defined as the time spent in recreation of the faculties of body, mind, and spirit. It is the surplus time that remains after all practical duties of life have been performed.

Since **leisure** has become as much a part of life as work, it needs fully as much consideration in our educational program. In fact, it needs more careful thought and planning since it, unlike work, has no outlined program to follow and no responsible "captain" for guidance except himself. In the prediction by Jacks,[1] that in a few years the average working time will be four hours per day, is to be fulfilled, then we shall see the advent of a new era in education in which entire institutions might have it almost as their sole aim of teaching the use of leisure hours. With the steady increase in machinery and man power, this prediction is likely to be fulfilled before the end of the twentieth century. If the working time of a group of a million men is reduced from eight to four hours each day in order to give work to another million unemployed persons, the amount of spare time would be the same, only it would be distributed. The need, therefore, of serious consideration of an educational program that teaches the use of leisure is self-evident.

The Danish people more than half a century ago began to realize the value of leisure hours. The charac-

---

[1] Jacks, "Ethical Factors of the Present Crisis," Chapter IV.

teristic Danish phenomenon—the People's College—became the educational movement for better living, while at work and play. "It may be said, too," May and Petgen write, "that Denmark has a conscious leisure movement, and that this movement is primarily educational in tendency.[1]

Considering the present social and economic conditions it seems advisable to teach wholesome recreations in **sports**. Such sports should not, if possible, be of the individual competitive type but rather as group competition, if competition at all. Group competition may have a wholesome psychological effect upon the individual student, as it teaches him the value and necessity of individual efforts in group efforts.

The Swedish and Danish systems of gymnastics, which are gradually developing into one system, consist of limb and body motions, jumping and rope-climbing, walking and running, and swimming. The object of such group gymnastics should be to give the mind control over the individual body in harmony with the motions of other individuals. Half an hour or one hour each day at gymnastics would serve as recreation for body development and control, and teach the meaning and value of cooperation.

A few years ago Danish gymnastics were introduced at the University of Iowa. It has proved a success among the students.

The advantage of gymnastics is not merely while in school but later in life. In practically every Danish farm community there is a gymnastic union. The participants are between the ages of sixteen and fifty. Often the union is divided into two groups—one for those less than thirty years of age and another for those from

---

[1] May and Petgen, "Leisure and Its Use," pp. 226-227.

thirty to fifty years. The practice is once a week and forms an important part of community education. The women have their separate organizations.

The courses of study should include the subjects of English grammar, American and World **literature,** and the art of expressing oneself clearly, freely, and correctly. Incorrect English is often a hindrance to individual progress. Acquaintance with the best literature in and outside America creates an interest in reading and aids in the ability to express oneself intelligently.

The study of mathematics should be considered practically and historically in order to show its connection with everyday usage. The history of mathematics will bring out the many fine uses to which mathematics lends itself. Many a student in Denmark has informed the writer that instead of "hating" mathematics they have come to "love" it by knowing its history and its practical uses. One semester might be devoted to the history of mathematics and one semester to its uses.

The **sciences** might include biology, botany, zoology, chemistry, and physics. These subjects should be viewed in their historical relation to human life. For the ordinary individual not many chemical formulas are necessary. Therefore, the application should be to everyday life.

Civics and **common** law are subjects with which every citizen shoul be familiar. These might be joined with the study of the political life in America since the time of Washington and even from the first settlement of America. The value of such a study would be in understanding the political conflicts of our own time.

A study of the **historical development of society** would bring the farm youth in contact with urban life and show the relation of urban life to rural life and vice versa. The subject of sociology is naturally related to economics to show the relationship between them.

It is difficult to say that one subject is more important than another as that depends largely upon the aim. But the founders of the People's College believed that **history** was the great unifying course which brought the present in contact with the past. At first Grundtvig gave history a romantic interpretation in showing the oneness of human history and the direct influence of God upon the characters who made history. Due to the influence of nationalism more stress is now given to modern times, often at the expense of ancient times. But most of the teachers in the People's Colleges maintain a balanced program in teaching ancient and modern history. The spiritual view of existence is retained. Special stress is laid on the study of great servants of God and fellow men. Grundtvig believed that history was largely the study of great men.

The study of great men and women in world history, and perhaps especially in national history, has an important psychological influence upon young lives which are easily stirred spiritually and emotionally. Young people have a tendency to enjoy the heroic side of life. America has had many **great men** of noble character who would serve as a fine inspiration to many young men and women. This need not be hero worship but merely a setting forth of good examples for future American citizens.

The study of great men has also a unifying and integrating effect upon young people, as it naturally centers many events and activities around one personality. Therefore, every subject which lends itself to historical interpretation in the light of great men, should be so interpreted.

To be historically-minded is an ability which should grow and develop throughout life. There is a constant need for the ability to search for truth, to demand evidence, to understand the dependence of the present on the past.

The story of man's marvelous progress along the road of civilization and culture is a thrilling one. As one studies the history of the race, one finds both material and industrial factors and the human and social qualities that have advanced civilization. Factors that have retarded progress will also be discovered. Crime, dishonesty, political corruption, and injustice are shown by history as negative elements in the improvement of social living, whereas the well-recognized social virtues are essential to human progress. The story of civilization, rightly interpreted, reveals those fundamental principles of human conduct and behavior that are essential to enjoyment of the highest culture of the present day and to participation in evolving a better culture for the succeeding generation.[1]

Cardinal Newman, in like manner, points to the importance of history when he says:

Again the study of history is said to enlarge and enlighten the mind, and why? Because, as I conceive, it gives a power of judgment of passing events, and of all events, and a conscious superiority over them, which before it did not possess.[2]

As already pointed out in a previous chapter, the **historical method of teaching** was recommended by Grundtvig. This method is used in all the People's Colleges of Denmark and has given satisfactory results. Both history and literature, and, in fact, all of the courses, should be taught with a more informal method of presentation. In order to make abstract statements concrete, applications should constantly be made wherever possible. The interest and attention of the student, which is of paramount importance for enlightenment,

---

[1] "Implications of Social-Economic Goals for Education," p. 47.
[2] Newman, "University Education," p. 124.

should be awakened, for only then can he truly understand a subject and apply it in life.

Although the school is not really a vocational school, practical courses that would be of use in the community might be taught, such as, courses in agriculture, bookkeeping and typing. Interest in hobbies and in keeping a diary should be developed. Such interests have a balancing effect upon the individual life.

Two or three evenings a week, open forums should be conducted by outside speakers or by the regular teachers. Some evenings might be devoted to motion pictures about foreign countries, making of paper, farm machinery, or national parks. The students should be given an opportunity to ask questions.

Singing, which is an excellent method of self-expression and at the same time inspirational, should be stressed in and out of the classroom. America is gradually developing a fine collection of songs which can be used profitably. The learning of songs in school may inspire men to sing at their work. Many a Danish farmer is heard singing as he ploughs his field.

Conclusion

The writer is of the firm conviction that a People's College, as herein outlined, would give opportunities to the many farm boys and girls who never finish high school or reach college. It is the farm youth who wish a non-technical and non-professional education that was in mind in writing this book. May a new day dawn for American farm youth.

It is fitting in closing to quote Mr. Hart, an American educator, who says:

America leads the world in psychology of the academic type. But America does not lead the world in understanding mind, especially the mind of youth. Yet, to **understand the mind of youth** is the gravest problem of our times. We face social issues that can never be solved without the discovery of new minds, and the only place where new minds capable of releasing new intelligence can be found is in the generation of youth. Hence, we shall do well to look closely into what other peoples have to teach us with respect to this most important of all our problems. And in this realm of understanding youthful mind, the Danes are preeminent.[1]

America has led the world in psychology of the academic type. Will it not wish in the future to lead also in the understanding of the mind of the farm youth? Will America take up the challenge?

[1] Hart, "Light From the North," p. 77.

THE FIGURE REPRESENTS THE ENLIGHTENMENT
OF THE DANISH PEOPLE

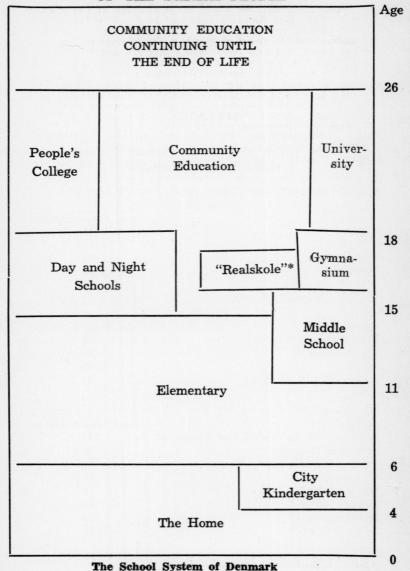

The School System of Denmark

*Business and Civil Service School

APPENDIX

Time Table Showing the Courses and the Number of Hours Given to Each in Various Divisions of the People's College[1]

I. Instruction in Danish in 25 People's Colleges
(Men)

Courses	Average Number of Hours
Reading	40
Grammar	43
Orthography	53
Themes	31

II. Instruction in History in 31 People's Colleges
(Men)

Courses	Average Number of Hours
Literature	42
Scandinavian	49
World	45
Church, Bible, Missions	47

III. Vocational Courses for Men (5 Months) (11 Colleges)

Courses	Average Number of Hours
Drawing and Geometry and Stereometry	143
Freehand Drawing	30
Professional Designing	218
Construction	59
Mathematics	6
Calculation	93
Bookkeeping	26
Natural Science	21

---

[1] "Statistiske Meddelelser." 4 Række, 104 Bind, 4 Hæfte, Folkehøjskoler og Landbrugsskoler, 1935-36. Pp. 24, 25.

Danish	128
History	88
Geography	19
Common Law	22
Singing	13
Reading	5
Gymnastics	72
Other courses	41

IV.   Courses at 12 Agricultural Colleges (5 months)
(Men)

Courses	Average Number of Hours
Natural Science	154
Study of Plants	159
Study of Livestock	179
Other Agricultural Subjects	150
Cultural Courses	339

V.   Courses at 7 Agricultural Colleges (9 months)
(Men)

Courses	Average Number of Hours
Natural Science	307
Study of Plants	272
Study of Livestock	322
Other Agricultural Subjects	354
Cultural Courses	369

VI.   Courses for Women in 39 People's Colleges
(3 months)

Courses	Average Number of Hours
Danish	102
Penmanship	3
Reading	25
History	101
Sociology	18
Geography	15
Physics	6
Chemistry	4
Zoology, Botany	16
Hygiene	20

Mathematics	53
Drawing	8
Singing	25
Gymnastics	67
Handwork	110
Domestic Science	22
Bookkeeping	6
Other Courses	47

VII. Instruction of Danish in 26 People's Colleges
(Women)

Courses	Average Number of Hours
Reading	28
Grammar	29
Orthography	36
Themes	20

VIII. Instruction in History in 27 People's Colleges
(Women)

Courses	Average Number of Hours
Literature	26
Scandinavian	29
World	27
Church, Bible Missions	31

Occupation of Parents of Students at People's Colleges and Agriculture Colleges for the Period 1935-36[1]

Sex	Number of Students	Farmers	Smallholders	Laborers	Artisans	Others
Men	5546	2475	671	406	397	1597
Women	3426	1617	423	124	322	940

Distribution of Ages of Students in the Period 1935-36[2]

Sex	Total Number of Students	Under 16	16-18 Years	18-25 Years	25 Years and Over	Ages Not Listed
Men	5546	3	110	3737	965	731
Women	3426	6	266	2629	287	138

[1] "Ibid.," p. 15.
[2] "Ibid.," p. 16.

Occupation of parents of students at People's and Agricultural Colleges for the period 1903 to 1915:[1]

Year	Number of Students	Farmers	Smallholders	Workers	Artisan	Professional
1903-04	7398	3758	1642	218	817	947
1904-05	7673	3936	1621	241	876	999
1905-06	7886	4154	1719	224	765	1024
1906-07	7660	4031	1669	214	746	1000
1907-08	7331	3682	1342	244	775	1088
1908-09	7917	4066	1742	255	775	1099
1909-10	8178	4294	1613	271	763	1237
1910-11	8257	4428	1675	250	798	1106
1911-12	8035	4326	1662	271	758	1018
1912-13	8038	4436	1533	282	1629	958
1913-14	8047	4386	1491	319	769	1082
1914-15	6830	3516	1342	299	748	925

Ages of students at People's and Agricultural Colleges during the years 1902-03 to 1914-15:[2]

Year	Total Students	Under 16 Years	16-18 Years	18-25 Years	Over 25 Years
1902-03	7361	72	520	5512	1132
1903-04	7398	68	554	5607	1159
1904-05	7673	50	562	5899	1162
1905-06	7886	62	534	6147	1143
1906-07	7660	46	539	6038	1037
1907-08	7331	43	468	5738	1082
1908-09	7917	58	541	6218	1090
1909-10	8178	41	449	6479	1209
1910-11	8257	43	515	6541	1158
1911-12	8035	41	504	6341	1149
1912-13	8038	64	531	6354	1089
1913-14	8047	47	524	6387	1089
1914-15	6830	52	470	5506	802

[1] Den Danske Folkehøjskole, p. 162.
[2] Ibid., p. 161.

BIBLIOGRAPHY

Alanne, V. S. *Fundamentals of Consumer Cooperation*. Northern States Cooperative League. Minneapolis, Minnesota. 1936.

Allport, Gordon W. *Personality a Psychological Interpretation*. Henry Holt. 1937.

Andersen, Olaf and Elling, M. *Fyn*. Andelsbogtrykkeriet. Odense. 1932.

Arnfred, J. Th. *Dansk Udsyn*. Jørgensen. Kolding. 1936.

Arnold, Mathew. *Irish Essays*. Macmillan. 1883.

Barfod, H. P. B. *Minder fra Gamle Grundtvigske Hjem*. Gads Forlag. Copenhagen. 1921. Vol. I, II, III.

Begtrup, Holger. *The Folk High Schools of Denmark*. Oxford University Press. London. 1926.

Bjerre, Siliam. *Dalum Landbrugsskole 1886-1936*. Andelsbogtrykkeriet. Odense. 1936.

Børneskolen. Department of Statistics. Copenhagen. 1934.

Breitwieser, J. V. *Psychological Education*. Alfred A. Knopf. 1926. Chapter XI.

Campbell, Mrs. Olive Arnold. *The Danish Folk High School*. Macmillan. 1928.

Carlyle, Thomas. *Past and Present*. Belford. Chicago. 1883.

Charters, W. W. *Teaching the Common Branches*. Houghton Mifflin. 1924. Pp. 176-218, 397, 398.

Childs, Marquis W. *Sweden The Middle Way*. Yale University Press. New Haven. 1936.

Christensen, Chris L. *Agricultural Cooperation in Denmark*. United States Department of Agriculture. Washington Bulletin 1266. 1924.

Christensen, George and Grundtvig, stener. *Breve fra og til N. F. S. Grundtvig.* Gyldendalske Boghandel. Copenhagen. 1924.

Den Danske Folkehøjskole. Udgivet af Foreningen for Højskoler og Landbrugsskoler. Schonbergske Forlag. Copenhagen. 1916.

Denmark. Published by the Danish Ministry for Foreign Affairs and the Statistical Department. Copenhagen. 1925. 1937.

Dewey, John, et al. *Implications of Social-Economic Goals for Education.* Committee National Education Association. Washington. 1937.

Douglas, Carl R. *Modern Methods in High School Teaching.* Houghton Mifflin. 1926. Pp. 163-167.

Emerson, Ralph Waldo. *Education.* Houghton Mifflin. 1909.

Englehart, Fred, and Overn, A. V. *Secondary Education.* Appleton-Century. 1937.

Finney, Ross L. *A Sociological Philosophy of Education.* Macmillan. 1928.

Fischer, E. E. *Social Problems.* The United Lutheran Publication House. Philadelphia. Chapter VII. 1927.

Foght, Harold W. *Rural Denmark and Its Schools.* Macmillan. 1915.

Folkehøjskolens Sangbog. Eksprestrykkeriet. Odense. 1913.

Folkehøjskoler og Landbrugsskoler samt Husholdningsskoler. 1931-1936. Department of Statistics. Copenhagen. 1937.

Fowler, Burton P. *The Educational Record.* What Is Important in Education? July, 1937.

Gladstone, William Ewart. *Gladstone and Palmerston, Correspondence.* Harper. 1928.

Goldmark, Josephine. *Democracy in Denmark.* National Home Library Foundation. Washington. 1936.

Greenbie, Marjorie B. *The Arts of Leisure.* McGraw-Hill Book Co., Whittlesay House. London. 1934.

Grimley, O. B. *The New Norway.* Griff-Forlaget, Oslo. 1937.

Grundtvig, N. F. S. *Christelige Prædikener.* Thieles Bogtrykkeri. Copenhagen. Volume I, II, III. 1895.

Digte. Steen og Son. Copenhagen. 1869.

Haandbog i Oldtidens Historie. Schonbergs Forlag. Copenhagen. Vol. I, II, III. 1867.

Harald Blaatand og Palnatoke. Schonbergs Forlag. Copenhagen. 1891.

Hyrde-Brevene. Reitzels. Copenhagen.

Kirkens Genmæle. Thieles Bogtrykkeri. Copenhagen.

Kirkelige Oplysninger. Tingnagels. Copenhagen. 1840.

Kirke-Spejl. Schonbergs Forlag. Copenhagen. 1876.

Kristelige Børnelærdom. Schonberg. Copenhagen. 1868.

Kristen-Livet. Lunos. Copenhagen. 1875.

Krønnike-Rim. Iversens Boghandel. Copenhagen. 1875.

Mands Minde. Schonbergs Forlag. Copenhagen. 1877.

Nordens Mythologi. Schubothes Boghandel. Copenhagen.
1870.

Paaske-Liljen. Iversens Boghandel. Copenhagen. 1882.

Hart, Joseph K. *Light From the North.* Henry Holt. 1926.

Hegland, Martin. *The Danish People's High School.* Bureau
of Education. Washington. Bulletin Number 45, 1915.

Hertel, H. *Andelsbevægelsen i Danmark.* Gyldendalske Boghandel. Copenhagen. 1917.

Hollman, A. H. *The Folk High School.* National Home Library Foundation. Washington, 1936.

Hollister, Horace A. *The Administration of Education in a
Democracy.* Scribner. 1914.

Holly, Charles Elmer. *The Practical Teacher.* The Century
Co. 1927. Pp. 164-170.

Howe, Frederic C. *Denmark—The Cooperative Way.* How-
ard-McCann. 1936.

Hutchins, Robert Maynard. *The Higher Learning in America.* Yale University Press. New Haven. 1936.

Jacks, L. P. *Ethical Factors of the Present Crisis.* Brown
University. Providence, R. I. 1934.

Jensen, Einar. *Danish Agriculture.* Schultz Forlag. Copenhagen. 1937.

Jensen, J. *Vort Fædrelands Historie.* R. Stjernholms Forlag. Copenhagen. 1895.

Jensen, Thyra. *Constance Leth. Grundtvigs Ungdomskærlighed.* Hagerups Forlag. Copenhagen. 1922.

Kierkegaard, P. Chr. *Om det nærværende Almue-Skolevæsen.* Reitzels Forlag. Copenhagen. 1849.

Koch, L. *Fra Grundtvigianismens of Den Indre Missions Tid.* (1848-1898). G. E. C. Gad. Copenhagen. 1898.

Kotsching, Walter M. *The Educational Record.* Limiting Student Enrollments. July, 1937.

Kuehner, Quency A. *A Philosophy of Education.* Prentice-Hall. 1936. Chapter XVIII.

Lynd, Robert S. and Lynd, Helen Merrell. *Middletown,* A Study in Contemporary American Culture. Harcourt, Brace and Co., 1929. Chapters XVII, XVIII, XIX.

Madsen-Vorgod, N. and Pinholt, J. Gr. *Landsbyskolens Læsebog.* Chr. Ericksens Forlag. Copenhagen. 1920.

Malmstrom, Johs. *Olfert Ricard, Minder og Optegnelser.* Frimodts. Copenhagen. 1933.

May, Herbert L. and Petgen, Dorothy. *Leisure and Its Use.* Barnes Co. 1928.

Mill, John Stuart. *Dissertations and Discussions.* Holt. 1882. Vol. I-V.

Newman, Cardinal John Henry. *On the Scope and Nature of University Education.* E. P. Dutton. 1915.

Ottosen, Johan. *Vor Historie.* "Frem." Det Nordiske Forlag. Oslo. 1902.

Overn, A. V. *The Teacher in Modern Education.* D. Appleton-Century Company. 1935.

People's College Bulletins:
    Den Udvidede Højskole i Haslev
    Haandværkerhøjskolen i Haslev
    Højskolen i Askov
    Tommerup Højskole i Knarreborg

Politikkens Aarbog. *Hvem, Hvad, Hvor.* Dagbladet. Politikken. Copenhagen. 1937.

Rosendal, H. *N. F. S. Grundtvig.* Hagerups Forlag. Copenhagen. 1923.

Ruskin, John. *Stones of Venice.* Alden. 1885.

Sandbæk, P. *Tommerup Højskole i 25 Aar.* Exprestrykkeriet. Odense. 1931.

Schrøder, Ludvig. Den Nordiske Folkehøjskole. Gads Forlag. Copenhagen. 1905.

Stefansson, J. *Denmark and Sweden—With Iceland and Finland.* T. Fisher Unwin. London. 1916.

Strayer, George Drayton and Norsworthy, Naomi. *How to Teach.* Macmillan. 1917. Chapter VIII.

Thwing, Charles F. *Education According to Some Modern Masters.* Platt and Peck. 1916.

United States Bureau of Education Publications:
Bulletin 1913, No. 58. *The Educational System of Rural Denmark.*

Bulletin 1914, No. 5. *The Folk High Schools of Denmark.*

Bulletin 1915, No. 22. *The Danish Folk High Schools.*

Bulletin 1914, No. 24. *Danish Elementary Rural Schools.*

Bulletin 1915, No. 45. *The Danish People's High School.*

Vig, P. S. *Danske i America.* C. Rasmussen Publishing Co. Minneapolis. 1908.

World Almanac 1938. New York World-Telegram. 1938.

Yearbook of Agriculture. Department of Agriculture. Washington. 1935.